Education That Works

James Bosco,

Beth Baker,

Glen Taylor

ISBN: 978-0-692-05655-4 (sc)
ISBN: 978-0-692-05722-3 (e)

Lulu Publishing Services rev. date: 07/27/2018

CONTENTS

ACKNOWLEDGMENTS

The authors acknowledge the excellent contributions of a number of people to the production of this book. Jennifer Hernandez, the W-A-Y Superintendent of Charter Schools and Madeline Black, the Director of Charter Schools, reviewed chapters of the book and made valuable suggestions. Jennifer Hernandez was quick to respond to questions and calls for help during the writing of the book with exactly what was needed. Michelle Sarkody, the Director of Compliance and Accountability, displayed her patience, friendliness, and competence in the face of many calls for help from the lead author. Bret Emil, Director of Development, was our "go-to" person for the details of the operation of the HERO, the W-A-Y Learning Management System. as well as a guide to the actual logistics and experiences of W-A-Y students as they proceed through the Program. Rebecca Straple, our copy editor demonstrated to us why she is considered invaluable as the Editor-in-Chief of the publications produced by the Western Michigan University Medieval Institute. The Design Center, Frostic School of Art at Western Michigan University provided the excellent book cover. The Art Director was Nick Kuder, and the Designer was Kailee McDade. Paul Sizer, the Production Manager and Assistant Director of the Design Center was unfailing helpful in moving us through the production of the cover to a very positive conclusion. The authors are most appreciative of the excellent final copy edit provided by Stephanie Carlson. If there was ever a case when last certainly is not least, we acknowledge the willingness of W-A-Y staff and students to participate in interviews that enables us to share the perspective on W-A-Y from the most important members of the W-A-Y community. Without their candor this book would have been far less than it is.

The Authors

INTRODUCTION

Making Education Work is a call to action for much needed school reform based on the work of two educators, Beth Baker and Glen Taylor. Beth and Glen are courageous educational leaders who do not just talk about breaking the mold, they are doing it. They have embraced innovation with all the opportunities and challenges that come with innovation. The transformed learning environment they have created is called W-A-Y for Widening Advancements for Youth.

W-A-Y is a project based, blended instruction, personalized learning program. Real change requires stepping away from policies and practices that may have worked in the past but are hindering our capability to get our schools to where they need to be. Tinkering around the edges will not do what needs to be done to provide a learning environment for the students we have in the world as it is. The success that W-A-Y has had is, in large measure, a result of the creation of it with very few "givens" that are incompatible with providing a best practice learning experience for its students. Beth and Glen have been in the educational trenches and know what our children want and need to be successful in this hyper-competitive, technologically-driven global economy where ideas and jobs can and do move around the globe effortlessly. It is preparing students to be successful for the world that is waiting for them.

In this book you will learn why and how Beth and Glen created W-A-Y. You will also learn how W-A-Y operates, meet W-A-Y students and staff members, and hear what they have to say about W-A-Y. The second chapter of the book provides information about the state of affairs in our schools. While W-A-Y is based in Michigan, by no means is the crisis facing our schools localized in just that one state. The last chapter of the book is a conversation with Beth and Glen about what they have learned in their work with W-A-Y, as well as their understanding of what needs to be done in moving forward.

When one talks to Beth and Glen it is quite clear that they do not consider W-A-Y as it exists today as the final approximation of it. Rather, they consider W-A-Y as a "work in progress." The two of them, and their highly dedicated staff, are committed to continuous improvement of W-A-Y. The motivation for this book was to share what they have learned with colleagues throughout the Nation who are similarly engaged in making the big changes in the school experience for our young people. They are committed to cooperating with individuals and educational organizations engaged in deep and wide educational reform that places students at the center of their work.

There is a tsunami coming with advances in automation and artificial intelligence that offers the potential for even greater disruption of traditional ways of work. Making Education Work provides a guide for how to ride this wave in a way that it will benefit our kids and nation. W-A-Y is continuing to grow nationally and internationally through the use of public and private partnerships. Tom Watkins

Tom Watkins, was president and CEO of the Economic Council of Palm Beach County Florida from 1996 to 2001. He also served as Michigan's State Superintendent of Public Instruction from 2001 to 2005. He has continued to be involved in issues and activities pertaining to the economy and education both in the U.S. and China.

ONE

The Path to W-A-Y

W-A-Y (Widening Advancements for Youth) was founded by two people who believed there was a critical need to provide a quality education for young people whose life situations or experiences in schools had jeopardized their education. They were deeply concerned about the large number of young people who were not getting the education they needed to live a productive and satisfying life. They considered this to be not merely a problem, but a crisis. This chapter tells the story of the path Glen Taylor and Beth Baker took that led to the creation of W-A-Y. To truly understand what W-A-Y is, it helps to know how it came to be.

WIDENING ADVANCEMENTS FOR YOUTH

W-A-Y is a 501(c)(3) non-profit corporation. The mission of W-A-Y is to change lives by creating engaging and encouraging educational opportunities for all young people. WAY offers a personalized approach to education; one that encourages self-esteem, independence, and the development of 21st century global and career skills. Currently there are 11 W-A-Y sites in Michigan with two types of campuses: Academies and Partner Sites. Academies are charter schools. They are autonomous educational entities that have been chartered by an organization authorized by the state of Michigan to do so. Universities, community colleges, intermediate school districts, and local school districts can establish a charter school. Charters are state public schools, but they are not under the aegis of any local school district; Charter schools have an appointed school board and become their own district. Thus, charter schools have much more flexibility to respond to students' life situations and needs than schools in a local education district. There are three W-A-Y Academies in Michigan. There is also one cyber school, named W-A-Y Michigan, which exists totally online. W-A-Y Partner Sites, on the other hand, are developed on a contractual basis with local school districts and work with schools within those districts. There are seven W-A-Y Partner campuses in Michigan.

W-A-Y Academies accept students from grades six to twelve, and these students receive diplomas from their Academy upon graduating; W-A-Y Partner Sites accept students from grades seven to twelve, and students receive diplomas from their local school districts rather than the Partner Site when they graduate.

W-A-Y sites are accredited by AdvancED, the largest community of educational professionals in the world. It is a non-profit, non-partisan, and non-governmental organization that conducts rigorous on-site external reviews of Pre-K-12 schools and school systems to ensure that all students realize their full potential. They accredit primary and secondary schools throughout the United States and internationally. It was formed in 2006 by the consolidation of the pre-college divisions of two of the U.S. regional accreditation organizations: The Commission on Accreditation and School Improvement of the North Central Association of Colleges and School, and the Council on Accreditation and School Improvement of the Southern Association of Colleges and Schools. AdvancED has given W-A-Y the highest level of endorsement. The AdvancED team felt that W-A-Y's accomplishments needed to be shared with a wider audience. The W-A-Y directors heard the same message from a State of Michigan assessment team that had visited W-A-Y. Like other successful projects, W-A-Y personnel were more committed to "doing it" than "talking about it."

So it was that this book was born, with the idea growing out of a conversation with AdvancED personnel following their most recent accreditation visit in 2017. The book tells the story of how W-A-Y came to be, what it is, and how it is making an important contribution to getting the education of our young people right. Beth Baker and Glen Taylor created W-A-Y, but when complimented for their vision they are quick to point out that W-A-Y's accomplishments can be attributed to their ability to find colleagues who shared their passion to make a positive change in the direction of the lives of the young people who have chosen W-A-Y for their education.

BETH AND GLEN BEGIN THEIR WORK AS EDUCATORS

Beth Baker and Glen Taylor both came from families of educators, but Beth did not initially choose education as a career. Instead, she earned a degree in public health and took her first job in a Detroit hospital, overseeing clinical education. In that job, she came to realize that education was the aspect of the job that brought her the most satisfaction. While still working at the hospital, she enrolled in a program leading to a teaching certificate. In 1990, she got her first job as an educator in a district in southeastern Michigan, aa permanent fourth grade substitute teacher. She was not off to a good start as an educator. In her words, "I had a horrendous year." The teacher she replaced left the job after experiencing a nervous breakdown, but the school administration hadn't recognized that she was having problems until several months into the school year. When Beth began her teaching job, her students had been taught by no fewer than five previous substitute teachers. Beth came to recognize that "no one seemed to know how to handle the situation, including me."

The difficulties posed by the situation were exacerbated by the behavior of the principal. As Beth explains, "I was a new teacher. This was my first assignment, and the principal didn't really know how to support new staff. She would try to be supportive by walking into the room and yelling at the kids to be quiet. Sometimes she would come over the overhead and yell at them to be quiet and to be respectful."

Beth and the principal had extremely different visions about what should be happening in the classroom: "The principal's vision was that the children would be sitting in rows and quiet, and my vision was that the children would be working in groups and talking, and because of the differences in our vision she wasn't able to support me when I needed assistance and I didn't know how to approach her to tell her what it was that I needed. And so, because of that, it was just, it was horrendous."

At the end of that year, Beth's teaching career appeared to be at an end. She decided to go in a different direction by starting her own business, called "Kid Smart Educational Services." Kid Smart was begun in response to the new problem of the growing capability for learning provided by the Internet contrasted with the inability of many schools to fully benefit from what educational technology had to offer because of a lack of resources. Kid Smart offered after-school and summer programs that integrated technology and collaborative learning and was used by a number of cities in their community centers. Initially the clientele for Kid Smart was students in kindergarten through seventh grade, but increasingly adults were also taking the classes that Kid Smart offered. When Beth sold the company after four years, the clientele was 40% young people and 60% adults.

After selling Kid Smart, Beth turned back to education. She enrolled in a master's program at Central Michigan University titled "Alternative Education in Non-Traditional Settings." Upon completing her degree in 1997, she took a job teaching third grade. This went far better than her first teaching job, and she realized she was meant to be an educator. Subsequently, the district moved her to sixth grade. and she held that position for four years. At the beginning of the 2005 school year, she was asked to join the staff of the Wayne County Regional Educational Service Agency (RESA) as their School Improvement and Curriculum Consultant.

Glen's career had fewer twists and turns than Beth's. He never seriously considered any career other than education: "I came from a family of teachers. Both my parents and my two sisters were teachers. My uncle was a superintendent. I wanted to be an elementary teacher from the beginning. I wanted to be involved working with kids, teaching and coaching." Upon graduating with a teaching certification, he became a volunteer at a large orphanage in Miacetlan, Mexico, near Cuernavaca, called Nuestros Pequenos Hermonos. Upon finishing his work at the orphanage, Glen taught for three years in Mexico at the American School Foundation of Guadalajara and then for one year in Xiamen China at the Xiamen International School. While teaching overseas, Glen earned a master's degree from Framingham State University in education. During his early career, he worked with children from very wealthy families, as well as those in impoverished situations. "Being in those countries, not as a tourist, but as a resident, was transformational. When I came back to the U.S. I realized I was looking at students and our public-school system with new eyes."

In 2001, he took a job as an elementary teacher in the Westwood Community School District in southeastern Michigan. After two years as a teacher, he became the principal of Daly Elementary School in the Westwood District. Leveraging his international experience, he started a Mandarin language program taught by native Chinese teachers and hosted by the Westwood school district. The opposition he faced in starting this program was a small foretaste of what he would later experience. He decided to continue his education with an educational specialist degree in educational policy and administration from Wayne State University. It was at Wayne State where Glen and Beth met and became colleagues in work that led to the creation of W-A-Y.

BETH AND GLEN MEET

Wayne RESA, which hired Beth in 2003, provides curriculum and instructional support as well as professional development for teachers in 33 local school districts in southeastern Michigan, including Detroit Public Schools.

Westwood Community Schools is one of the districts served by Wayne County RESA, but it was not because of that connection that Beth and Glen began their work together. Rather, both entered the educational specialist program at Wayne State University at the same time and were by happenstance placed in classes together. It quickly became clear to them that they shared strong convictions about the need to respond to the drop-out crisis. They both were convinced that more and better efforts were needed to respond to the crisis.

When they met, both had responsibility for obtaining state and federal funding to address curriculum and instruction problems and needs. Beth was working with schools with low student achievement levels and assisting them in developing school improvement plans and winning grant funding to implement the improvements. One of the issues being faced by Wayne RESA—and many other school organizations—was the consequence of the disconnect of technology from curriculum. Even though there was lots of talk about the connection between technology and curriculum, the organizational structure did not match the talk. In Wayne RESA and in many of the school districts it served, technology and curriculum were overseen by separate departments. Although Beth was a curriculum specialist, she was placed in the instructional technology department of Wayne RESA to generate better linkage between the two departments. Her mission was to help school personnel integrate digital media assets into their work to make substantial improvements in learning. Beth realized that computers were not the "silver bullet," but if used effectively, instructional technology could be a vital component in an innovative approach to creating a learning environment program that could put young people who were at risk of being lost on a much better path. Ultimately, digital media would play a key role in W-A-Y.

When Glen became principal of Daly Elementary School he was also assigned the responsibility of managing the district's efforts to secure state and federal projects. This was a district-wide responsibility, and Glen had close contact with secondary education in the district as a result. He was troubled by what he saw in the other middle schools and the high school in the district. In his words, "I was an elementary school principal. I got to see those great, beautiful kids who did well in school, and scored well on tests, and who enjoyed being in school. They get into middle school and suddenly they're getting into trouble. If they make it to high school, they're now labeled as problem kids." He knew he needed to do something about this, and he committed himself to making a positive difference in the lives of young people who were not being served by their schools. In 2008, Glen was recognized nationally in Washington, D.C. for his work with at-risk youth.

The district high school was facing two problems: One was a financial deficit and crisis within the district; the other was a growing recognition that something needed to be done to address the problem of students who were disengaged from school. Each one of those students was seriously in danger of dropping out of school. Some in the community and administration were more concerned with the first problem or the second one, but the two problems were actually tightly linked.

7

Glen found the adoption of project based learning an excellent means for addressing both of those problems. Project based learning (PBL) is an approach to learning in which students gain knowledge and skills by researching an authentic and challenging question or problem. The culmination of the student's work in a PBL experience is a product that makes use of the knowledge and skills they have gained rather than performance on a test. The use of projects as a learning resource is not new, yet, as we will see in the next chapter, projects are not often the main learning resource in schools. In recent years, the power of project based learning has been substantially augmented using digital media that greatly expands the learning resources and process for producing the desired results.

Beth reflected on the appeal of PBL. "It's really not a big jump for elementary teachers and elementary principals to appreciate project based learning because they already know and see that learning is connected. And good teachers in elementary schools already are connecting project learning with the way they're delivering instruction in their classrooms to keep kids engaged and to avoid isolating the curriculum subject by subject."

From a different vantage point, Beth was seeing the same problems as Glen: "I looked at the dropout crisis and said, 'Now, what can we do? What kind of solutions can we develop? I began exploring how we could use grants for networking of teachers not just within our RESA districts, but statewide. With a grant I was able to start a PBL initiative. It was called 'Leading Project based Learning.' The program was eventually retitled and absorbed by 'Michigan Champions,' which was a state-wide initiative to bring teachers together to learn in a collaborative way to create an inventory of projects for a project based learning initiative." The intent of this workshop was to build a large library of projects that would be peer-reviewed and could be improved by using Wikispaces for teacher collaboration. Michigan Champions attracted considerable attention.

Beth's experience in creating the project based learning network was very valuable for the work Beth and Glen would do together, it gave them knowledge and experience in creating and using project based learning in multiple sites. The two of them became partners in creating the Cyber School. While PBL was a critical component of the School, it was only one of the structural and organizational changes embodied in the Cyber School. This would prove to be valuable knowledge since W-A-Y would also occupy multiple sites.

When Beth and Glen began working together their intent was not to create a new school; rather, they saw their task as making use of grant resources to promote change and to improve school practices in the schools where they were working. They visited schools which were widely considered to be innovative and successful, such as New Tech High in Napa, California and High Tech High in San Diego. They realized there were people in other schools who were moving in the direction they wanted to go. It made sense to learn all that could be learned from what was working in those schools.

ENTER JEAN JOHNSON AND JONNY DYER

It was in presenting work on the Wayne RESA at a national conference sponsored by the Consortium for School Networking (CoSN) in Washington, D.C. that Beth and Glen met Jean Johnson and Johnny Dyer. Jean and Jonny were based in England. Jean began her career in East London schools, working with difficult and disaffected teenagers. She was charismatic and hearing her talk about her efforts to help the "street kids" of London was inspiring to Beth and Glen. Jean was a pioneer in the use of new technologies and was an early adopter of the use of the Internet for schools. She was involved in several high profile online projects in the UK, Sweden, Finland, USA, India, Japan, and New Zealand. Jonny Dyer worked at Ultralab based at Anglia Ruskin University in Chelmsford,

Essex, U.K. His work was focused on the use of technology for learning. In 2000, Jean and Jonny created the NotSchool Project, which was focused on social inclusion for disadvantaged youth, with an emphasis on the creative and innovative use of multimedia to develop learning. The goal of NotSchool was to demonstrate that young people for whom 'school does not fit' can renew their confidence in learning and gain a range of qualifications that recognize their progress.

The approach being used by Jean and Jonny made use of PBL in an online environment. Given what Beth and Glen were doing it was not surprising that their paths crossed at the CoSN meeting. Beth remembers Jean telling them, "This is what we've done. It works well. It has engaged kids that are at risk." What was evident to Beth and Glen was that Jean and Jonny had a way to communicate with kids online that worked really well. Their approach was informal and underplayed any status difference between the teacher and the student. Thus, the appeal of NotSchool to Glen and Beth was that PBL was working effectively with young people who were like those that they wanted to reach.

So it was that Glen and Beth decided to go to London to get a firsthand look at NotSchool. They were particularly impressed by the manner in which the NotSchool personnel communicated and interacted with their students. While there were aspects of NotSchool that would not fit with the U.S. situation, they liked what they saw, and what they saw in London solidified their sense that PBL could provide the basic structure for the conduct of learning in the program they would develop. In one very important way, NotSchool was different than what W-A-Y would become: NotSchool was totally online. Except for W-A-Y Academy, W-A-Y would make use of a blended learning approach, incorporating both online learning as well as learning on site. It was clear to both Glen and Beth that NotSchool, as it was functioning in England, would not be appropriate for what they felt was needed in the U.S. NotSchool was functioning as a research project, Beth and Glen's intent was to build a fully functioning school. As Glen and Beth considered the various programs and approaches they had seen in the U.S. and the U.K., along with what they had learned from them, it was quite clear that attempting to fit the change and innovation that was needed into existing schools would provide only limited success. Instead, a new form of schooling, with a new organizational structure and a culture that was very different than the typical high school, had to be created.

CREATION OF WESTWOOD CYBER SCHOOL

Not long after Glen and Beth came back from London, they presented a proposal to the Westwood School District Board to establish a Cyber School. The clientele for the school would be students who had dropped out or who were likely to drop out of school. PBL was to be the approach used to accomplish the learning objectives required to earn a high school diploma in Michigan. However, Glen and Beth realized that PBL did not represent the totality of what was needed to make the school work for the students. It was only a part – although an important part – of what was needed to make the Cyber School effective for the students it was created to serve. It would not work if Cyber School operated like a conventional high school with PBL dropped into the mix. Westwood Cyber School, like NotSchool, would not be just a somewhat revised version of the traditional high school. Beth and Glen intended that students in the Westwood Cyber School should realize quickly that the Cyber School was not like the other high school(s) they had attended.

Getting approval to develop the school occurred over five board meetings. Beth and Glen had to respond to many questions and concerns. Some of the opposition from school personnel was focused on the use of PBL in the school. Yet the objections to the proposed Cyber School went beyond the use of PBL: Since the Cyber School was making transformational changes in how teaching and learning occurred as well as in the role of students and staff and how they interacted, it was not surprising that there was opposition to it. Glen and Beth heard from some personnel who believed that their approach would work with gifted students, but those critics argued that the clientele of the Cyber School needed more structure and teacher direction. Some who recognize that the traditional structure and teacher-student role is not working in schools think that the solution to these problems is to tighten the existing structure and provide less tolerance for student autonomy. Ironically, it would have been more problematic had the Board found it easy to approve the formation of the new school; had that been the case, it would have meant that Beth and Glen were not really deviating much from existing school methods and structures, which they believed needed to drastically change.

There were issues facing the school district that made the Cyber School attractive to the board. One was that a neighboring school district had begun bussing, and there was attrition from Westwood because of the convenience bussing would provide for parents. Thus, one incentive for school officials for creating the Cyber School was to create a new school that hopefully would draw students to Westwood.

One Board member, who was a business man, became a committed and effective advocate. He was respected by the board members and his support was pivotal. The board finally agreed to a pilot with a target of 180 students. In 2007, Westwood Cyber School began, and the doors of the school opened to students in the following year. The Cyber School was housed in a modular building behind Daly Elementary School. Glen left the principalship at Daly Elementary School and became the Executive Director of Innovation as well as the principal of the Westwood Cyber School, while retaining his responsibility for state and national programs within the Westwood district. Beth remained in her job at the RESA and continued working with Glen as a co-director of the Cyber School.

Beth and Glen had no way of knowing what the response of the parents and students would be to the Cyber School. It was far from certain that they could attract the target 180 students. They advertised the Cyber School county-wide and reached the target at the time of the opening of the School. Most of the students who enrolled came from districts in Wayne County, but outside Westwood.

State funding for public schools is determined by the "first Friday count." Districts report the student population in their schools on the first Friday of the school year. The student population of the Cyber School grew to 540 in the first six months of its operation, which produced a 33% increase in enrollment in the Westwood District. The 33% increase in district student population when the Cyber School resulted in a substantial increase in state funding. While the driving force for Beth and Glen in creating the Cyber School was not increasing state funding to the Westwood School District, they realized that the increase in state funding was a factor that led some school authorities to look favorably on the Cyber School.

It quickly became clear that the school was meeting a need. Nevertheless, the school was not without its critics. Criticisms took various forms. Glen recalls "Some flak came from the fact that we were providing students in the Cyber School with computers in their home. This was met by some with considerable hostility. I remember janitors that were helping unload the machines into the Cyber School swearing and cussing, saying, 'You're gonna give these damn kids computers?'" Beth had a similar experience: "When we started the W-A-Y network, I had the computers delivered to my house. The FedEx guy wasn't happy that we were giving computers to kids that already had a chance." As we will see in the next chapter, there lots of statements about the need to provide students who have left school with a good opportunity to complete their high school education, there was also lots of grass roots opposition from both school personnel and citizens to committing resources to kids that "should've done it right the first time, they already had a chance!"

W-A-Y IS BORN

The success of the Cyber School caused leaders in other districts to be interested in opening a similar site within their own district. In 2009, Glen and Beth, still in their jobs at the Westwood District and the Wayne County RESA, opened two sites elsewhere in the state at the behest of the Michigan Department of Education. These sites were the first to be named "W-A-Y": the acronym for "Widening Advancements for Youth."

It was clear that there was a need for the type of education that Cyber School was providing, and Beth and Glen were being contacted by other districts interested in hosting a site. They both faced difficult personal decisions: At that time Glen was serving in the Westwood District as Executive Director of Innovation and State and Federal Programs.

Should they remain in their current positions with Wayne RESA and Westwood Community Schools and confine the benefits of W-A-Y to a limited audience, or should they leave their current positions to make it possible to reach more young people who could benefit from W-A-Y? Both had families and they had to weigh very carefully the potential consequences on their families if the W-A-Y venture failed. In 2009, they both decided to leave their current jobs, and W-A-Y was established as a non-profit corporation with Beth and Glen as the co- executive directors. The Cyber School in the Westwood District remained and is still functioning.

There have been bumps in the path. Challenges remain, but both Beth and Glen are certain that the decision to focus their professional work on widening advancement for young people who otherwise may well have been left behind was the right one.

Reflecting on the journey to the creation of W-A-Y, Beth explained: "We've had a lot of success upfront, and had lots of people interested in what we were doing, but it's not the only way that it can be done to get the same effect. If you asked us, do we have this secret sauce even now, I would say 'no.' We have what we constructed as it is now, but we're always looking to see how we can make it better. When we believe we have THE answer we should probably leave the job."

In the next chapter we will take a step back and examine the educational context within which W-A-Y was established. The problem that Beth and Glen were addressing in southeast Michigan was not just a local problem. Nationally, far too many young people in the U.S. were not being served adequately by their high schools. This was true even though there was good information available about how the nations' schools could do a much better job in meeting their needs.

TWO

Educating America's Youth: Challenges and Opportunities

In the fall of 2016, over fifty million students began the school year in U.S. public schools. Another six million were in private schools. It is far from merely a cliché to say that they are America's future. There is no question more important to our nation than this: How well are we providing for the education of our youth? There is sharp disagreement about the answer to that question. A few minutes of surfing on the Internet brings the flavor of the debate about the quality of U.S. schools into focus. The surfer will find articles with titles such as these: "American Schools Are Failing," "An Indictment of Education: Why Are Our Schools Failing Us?" and "How the U.S. Education System is Failing Our Youth." Yet, the exploration of the Internet will also reveal titles on the other side of the issue, such as: "The Myth of Public School Failure," "America's Education System is Not Broken," and "Why U.S. Schools are Simply the Best". The dialogue between critics and proponents of public education is not terribly helpful. It is considerably more useful to acknowledge that we can—and must do better and do all we can to make the best use of the knowledge of scholars and the work of skilled practitioners who can guide us on the path toward significant improvement.

MANY OF OUR YOUTH ARE BEING LEFT BEHIND

Whether one liked or disliked the George W. Bush administration's agenda for elementary and high school education, the name of the legislation, "No Child Left Behind," identified a commendable goal. Far too many of our young people are being left behind. The graduation rate for public schools in the U.S. in 2014 was 82%.[1] This is a three percent increase from 2011.[2] Any improvement in the on-time graduation rate is welcome news, but it is troubling that one in five young people will not graduate on time, and a substantial percentage of them will never achieve a diploma at all.

The graduation rate for states in 2014 varies considerably, from 91% in Iowa to 69% in New Mexico. Also, the graduation rate of school districts within a state can be widely discrepant. Data for school districts in New Mexico, a state with a 69% graduation rate that publishes graduation rate by district, shows a considerable range, with three 3 districts reporting a 98% graduation rate and two districts reporting a 64% rate. The graduation rates for other districts in the state are distributed between those two points.[3] This wide disparity of graduation rates among school districts in New Mexico is not unique to that state.

The low graduation rate is a particularly serious problem in many of our cities. Sixteen of the nation's 50 largest cities had a 2013 graduation rate lower than 50% in the school district serving the city. Those with the lowest graduation rates include Indianapolis (31%), Cleveland (34 %), Detroit (38 %), Milwaukee (41%), Baltimore (41%), Atlanta (44 %), Los Angeles (44 %), Las Vegas (45 %), and Columbus (45 %).[4] 2013 graduation rates for the various sub-groups of students vary greatly: Asian and white students had a graduation rate of 89% and 87%, respectively; the graduation rate for Latinos was 76%; for African-Americans the rate was 73%; for American Indians the rate was 70%; and for students with disabilities, the graduation rate was 63%.[5]

The on-time graduation rate for Michigan students in 2013 was 77%. This puts Michigan in the lower half of U.S. states, with a rank of 33.5%. Michigan is under the U.S. mean graduation rate for all of the five following sub-groups: American Indian, 64% (6% lower than the U.S. mean); Asians, 87% (2% lower than the U.S. mean); Whites, 82% (5% lower than the U.S. mean); Latinos, 67% (9% lower than the U.S. mean); and African Americans, 61% (10% lower than the U.S. mean). As the above paragraph indicates, there are only two cities (Cleveland and Indianapolis) among the 50 largest U.S. cities that had a lower graduation rate than Detroit.[6]

The large number of young people who drop out of school and never achieve a high school diploma is a critical national problem. One of the national consequences of all these students dropping out of school is the cost to the national economy. A Seattle Times report put it this way:

> Of 40 million Americans between 16 and 24, about 6.7 million are neither in school nor employed. About half are high school dropouts; the others may have a GED. All are underemployed, if they work at all. To taxpayers, each of these so-called "opportunity youths" imposes a lifetime cost of about $235,680 in welfare payments, food stamp, criminal justice and medical care. Multiply that across the full 6.7 million cohort and the hit is nearly incomprehensible: $1.6 trillion.[7]

The National Center for Educational Statistics reported that the mean salary for young adults between the ages of 25 and 34, without a diploma, who work full time, was $23,900. This puts those persons at only $8,170 above the U. S. poverty level for a family of two, and only $50 over the poverty level for a family of four.[8]

There is another, less obvious consequence of the dropout problem: The Centers for Disease Control and Prevention (CDC) contends that dropouts comprise a public health problem:

> If medical researchers were to discover an elixir that could increase life expectancy, reduce the burden of illness, delay the consequences of aging, decrease risky health behavior, and shrink disparities in health, we would celebrate such a remarkable discovery. Robust epidemiological evidence suggests that education is such an elixir. Yet health professionals have rarely identified improving school graduation rates as a major public health objective, nor have they systematically examined their role in achieving this objective. Seizing the opportunity to do so can improve health and reduce disparities.[9]

Just as there is a cost for bringing the right resources to bear on solving the problem, there is a very high cost to the nation as a consequence of the high number of students who fail to get a high school diploma. Moreover, the nation loses the talent and energy that those young people could bring to the good of the nation.

Our young people are not merely economic statistics. The goal of every educator and every contentious policy maker should be to take the steps necessary so that every American young person can have a good, productive and satisfying life. Knowing what is known about the consequences of students dropping out of school for the individuals, it is unconscionable to fail to define the problem as a major national priority with the concomitant commitment of human and fiscal resources to solve the problem.

Some people may feel that it is inevitable that a substantial number of young people will leave school every year without a diploma. As we shall see, some school practices are far too responsible for students dropping out of school. In a *Los Angeles Times* article, Cynthia Parsons the editor of *Vermont Schoolhouse*, wrote about "Dropout Darwinism." This refers to the practice of school counselors who focus on "helping the fittest [and] abandoning the rest."[10] Unfortunately, too often teachers, administrators, and counselors "give up" on students who are at the periphery of the school. Effective resources need to be available to help students get back on track while they are in school, or good options for them to achieve a diploma if they have left their school need to be offered. Every one of the young people who begins his or her after-school life without a diploma counts as one more person in the unacceptably high number of those who have been left behind.

In a 2013 study conducted in the Midwest, teachers were interviewed to obtain their opinions of the causes of students dropping out of school. The study found that a substantial percentage of teachers felt rather powerless to do anything about the drop-out crisis. In the words of the authors of the study:

> Teachers' perceptions of the causes of dropout tended to focus on factors outside of their control. Factors that support strong student-teacher relationships were more moderately rated as contributing to dropout. A quarter of the teachers reported that they had only limited influence on students' decisions to stay in or dropout of school.[11]

If school personnel conclude that the problem with disenfranchised students is a result of factors beyond their control, the opportunity for that school to be a constructive factor in reducing the dropout rate or in providing other school approaches to provide a second chance at a diploma for those who have dropped out is seriously diminished. This is so even if the district has proclaimed an effort to reduce the dropout rate.

Writing in the Hechinger Report, Nina Rees put it this way:

> We should be doing everything we can to ensure that every student earns a high school diploma. That includes setting aside the notion that the traditional high school model works for every student. Students learn in many ways, and by the time they're in high school, teenagers are developing their own passions and interests that will shape how they view school and how they prepare for life. In a world of seemingly limitless choices, it doesn't make sense to try to force all students into the same academic box.[12]

Many educators and policy makers who are concerned about the quality of American public education have led efforts to raise curriculum standards and improve standardized test scores. Certainly, calling for the highest level of accomplishment that our young people can achieve is a good thing, but raising standards and enforcing accountability through standardized testing is unlikely to produce good results without effective changes in the teaching and learning environment. Indeed, in one regretful sense, district success is enhanced by low-achieving students dropping out of school, since their scores will no longer be included in the school's success statistics. As one examines the "higher standards" movement around the nation, the instances where there is a credible plan for actually accomplishing these higher standards are rare. Students whose connection to the school is precarious are particularly vulnerable to the risks of raising standards without an action plan to accomplish this goal.

It is quite important to keep in mind that the real task of education is not simply to enable the student to get a diploma. If that was the goal, the facile means to reach the goal would be to turn high schools into diploma mills. Obviously, the easy solution is not the right solution. Lowering standards would result in higher graduation rates, but such an action would, in effect, "throw in the towel" in enabling the student to get a diploma but failing to put the student on track to get an education that leads to a productive career and life. Arizona's Grand Canyon Diploma is an example of an initiative that is intended to raise graduation rates by lowering graduation standards.[13] That approach is better for state statistics than it is for the students it is intended to serve. Ultimately, what the world beyond the schools wants from young people is not merely their ability to be successful test-takers; rather, the world needs citizens who bring fresh energy and productive competencies to their jobs and communities.

There are serious academic and civil efforts at the state and local districts level in response to the dropout problem throughout the United States. There are many dedicated teachers, administrators, philanthropists, and private citizens who are doing good work on behalf of young people who otherwise would be abandoned. National organizations such as the National Dropout Prevention Center, the National Education Association, the National Alternative Education Association, and America's Promise Alliance are four of the prominent non-profit organizations that are providing support to districts and individuals who understand the serious nature of the dropout problem and who are acting to help solve the problem. It is not that nothing is being done; it is that *more* needs to be done.

A FRAMEWORK FOR UNDERSTANDING THE PROBLEM

The first step in solving a problem is understanding the problem. Fortunately, there is ample, good knowledge available to help us understand why students leave school without a diploma. Knowledge, rather than opinion and conjecture, provides the most secure foundation for the design of effective programs for students who are at risk of not attaining a diploma.

If a doctor is treating a patient with a medication that is not working, he or she has one critical insight that can guide his or her efforts to cure the patient: The doctor knows what doesn't work. That is quite valuable information in the process of developing and refining the treatment. A doctor who continues to treat a patient with a drug that has been shown to be non-efficacious for that patient would be guilty of malpractice. Too often, the approach to dealing with a student who is at risk of dropping out of school is focused on repeating practices that have not worked, rather than on making responsive changes to the factors that are jeopardizing the student's likelihood of graduation.

One of the most valuable research studies for understanding the dropout problem was produced by Jordan and colleagues.[14] Their research found "push" and "pull" factors that cause the student to leave school. "Push" factors are circumstances in the school that have a negative impact on students' engagement with the school program and influence them to leave school. Yet, as Jordan et al. observed, school is only one aspect of the student's world; in contrast to push factors, "pull" factors are conflicts between the school requirements and other aspects of the student's life that may "pull" him or her from the school. When students are pulled from school by some event or problem in their life, their departure may occur without any warning signs. For those students who are pushed from school, dropping out of school is generally not a sudden event or irrational decision; rather, it is the result of a cumulative process. The student's disengagement or alienation from school is generally conspicuous to those school personnel who care to look.

In a 2013 comprehensive analysis of seven nationally representative surveys of students who dropped out of school, Doll and colleagues examined the specific factors that pushed or pulled students from school and produced a comprehensive list of the factors.[15] Examples of push factors were: the young person missed too many school days; did not feel he or she belonged there; was failing; could not get along with teachers; etc. Examples of pull factors were: the young person needed to support the family; became pregnant; had to care for a family member; etc. The literature on push/pull factors makes it quite clear that it is a mistake to stereotype the dropout student. The factors that affect the student's disposition to school vary among students. Consequently, one size—or one approach—does not fit all!

Solving the dropout problem requires two types of programmatic responses. One is to develop effective school practices and programs to keep students who are headed toward school disengagement *in* school by addressing the factors that are pushing them out. The Center for Public Education, an organization created by the National School Boards Association, produced a comprehensive review of research that highlights concrete actions school districts can take to substantially reduce dropout rates and enable a higher number of students to graduate with a diploma. It specifies the actions and processes that districts must do, and must do well, to make major progress on helping students complete high school.[16]

The Center for Public Education report recognizes that dropping out of school is, in many instances, a predictable event. Intervention that is attempted as the student is getting ready to exit is likely to be too late. Yet, it is not enough for school personnel to be aware that a student is likely to drop out of school; the school needs to be able to intervene in a way that is responsive to the problematic situation confronting the student. The report also makes it clear that the intervention needs to be personalized.

While some contend that racial factors, socioeconomic status, age of the student at matriculation, and gender disproportionately affect dropout rates, the Center for Public Education report provides research that shows variations in school dropout rates even when controlling these variables. The report makes it clear that schools are far from impotent when it comes to making significant improvements to their ability to retain students. There is both an economic incentive to do this, since schools receive state funding based on the number of students in the district, and an ethical imperative to not abandon the young people entrusted to educators without doing all they can to make school work for them.

The second programmatic response to the dropout problem pertains to the students who have left school. Even if high schools have good practices and programs in place for at-risk students, some students will leave the school. This could be a result of pull factors, or because those students have reached a point where they conclude that leaving school is their only good option. In such instances, they have passed the "point of no return" with their school. Even schools that have the student's best interest at heart may be unable to make some of the needed accommodations because of logistical or policy constraints. Thus, even with the right things happening in the high school program, there will continue to be a need for educational agencies to offer opportunities for students who have left school to obtain their high school diploma.

Just as there are diverse reasons why students leave school, there are diverse reasons why students stay in school. Some students feel good about school and are engaged in their studies. Some students stay in school because of parental pressure. Some students, even those who may not be feeling positive about their work in the school, accept the fact that they need a diploma as a means to an end and they are willing do what they need to do to get it. Such students who stay in school may not actually see their school situation differently from those who leave.

In 2015 the Born this Way Foundation and the Yale Center for Emotional Intelligence surveyed 22,000 high school students about their high school experience. The results of the survey were clear and quite disconcerting. When students were asked how they feel in school, approximately 75% of the words they used were negative; only 23% of the descriptions were positive. The top three emotions the students reported feeling about high school were "tired" (39% of the respondents), "stressed" (29%), and "bored" (26%).[17]

An Aspen Institute that was based on several large-scale surveys of high school students provided details on the perspectives of high school students toward their high school experience:

- One-quarter (24%) of all high school graduates, including 26% of all current college students and 20% of non-college students, say that they faced high academic expectations and that they were significantly challenged in high school.
- More than half (56%) of all high school graduates faced moderate expectations, whereas one in five (20%) found that expectations were low and that it was easy to slide by.
- Less than one third (29%) of high school students report that they are excited about their classes.
- Less than half of high school students report that their school work makes them curious to learn about other things.[18]

The question of the accuracy or legitimacy of the opinions in the Aspen Institute report might well be raised. That is a fair question. However, in an important sense, it is the opinion that matters more than the reality. Those students make it clear that the students who drop out are not the totality of high school students who are not having a good experience in school. There is good reason to believe that what works for young people who have left school represents best practice and would actually be beneficial for students who remain in school and graduate as well.

There is a saying that emerged in early 18th century Germany that has been used by some schools as a motto. In Latin it reads: *Non scholae sed vitae.* The English translation is: "We learn not for school but for life." It is not enough to have students leave the school with a diploma in their hands. They need to leave school with realistic hopes, plans, knowledge, and competencies to build a good future for themselves and to contribute to the social and economic well-being of their country.

WHAT WORKS? DESIGNING A SOLUTION

Too frequently, those designing a solution to a problem must start with givens: Their task is to design the solution with and around existing structural features that must be kept in place. This is also generally the case for those seeking to innovate in schools. Every school exists within a context of federal, state, and local laws, customs, and policies, many of which are quite sacrosanct. This means that even creative and dedicated teachers and administrators must frequently settle, not for the necessary, but for the possible. The design of an educational environment that provides substantial aid to young people who have left school before graduating needs to start with a clean slate. Thus, the design and development process of such an environment is more like building a completely new structure than renovating an existing one.

At the core of making education work for young people who have not fared well in their previous schools is the establishment of a new school culture. School culture is "the beliefs, perceptions, relationships, attitudes, and written and unwritten rules that shape and influence every aspect of how a school functions." [19] In effect, school culture represents the totality of the human environment of the school. This includes what is permissible and non-permissible for students' behavior, the extent of formality/informality in day-to-day activities, the way in which teachers communicate and interact with students, and the specific nature of the roles of teacher and student. It needs to be clear that both the teacher and the student are on the same side rather than it being teacher vs. student. It is easy for educators to make statements such as, "I am here to support my students' learning;" but it is the concrete actions toward creating an improved school culture rather than just saying the right words that truly matter.

There is no doubt that inept teachers and administrators can create a dysfunctional school culture, but it is often the case that the structural aspects of the school—the givens of the school situation—hinder the establishment of positive and productive relationships. Even dedicated and competent teachers are severely compromised when they face rules and regulations that are inimitable to a quality learning environment. The number of students assigned to a teacher, the segmentation of the school day into fifty or so minutes for a class, the course content that requires the teacher to not spend too much time on any student who "isn't getting it," are all factors that may prevent teachers who have the capacity and motivation to form more healthy and positive relationships with their students from doing so.

Earlier in this chapter, we referred to a doctor who would be guilty of malpractice if she or he continued the use of a treatment that the doctor knew was not effective for the patient. Despite many advances in medicine, in some instances there may be no effective medication for a patient's illness. Fortunately, there is a much better situation for those working to make the school experience effective for young people who have not responded to the prior "treatment;" who have studied these issues and, who are cited below, have identified six elements that should be incorporated into the school culture in order to better serve students who are at risk of leaving school without a diploma. The fact that much of this research is not new is distressing, since it indicates that too often educators and policy makers in the U.S. have ignored or been unaware of research at their disposal which could improve the lives of so many young people for whom traditional schooling models are insufficient.

The six elements are as follows:

A clear separation from the traditional high school. The student needs to see the new school environment as really a *new* environment. Just making cosmetic modifications to the existing environment, even if done as an effort to respond to the student's needs, does not work. Tuck found that 75% of students who have dropped out of school and return to the school a year later drop out again. The challenge of succeeding in the same environment where they have experienced failure is difficult for most students to accomplish.[20] The difference in the school environment, then, should not be subtle or require time to recognize. It should be apparent to students when they enter their new school.

A non-competitive environment. It is important that the new school be characterized by a lack of competition among students. Student success should be measured by the student's own awareness of his or her personal growth rather than simply by tests or grades. The constraint on improvement, if any, should not be a consequence of the rules and procedures of the school.[21] Much less emphasis should be put on achievement test scores as an indicator of student success, with more emphasis being put on concrete and discernable accomplishment of competencies.

A small ratio of students to teachers. Even teachers who are committed to working closely with their students cannot do so if the ratio of students to teachers is high. In a traditional high school classroom environment where the teacher works through presentation to the entire class, size is less of a problem. Yet, if the role of the teacher is to be a learning coach for the student, the number of students that teachers must serve should not be excessive, as is often the case in U.S. high schools. Moreover, a healthy personal relationship between the teacher and the student, which is the antidote for a major "push" factor leading to drop-outs, can only occur if the teacher has the right amount of time to spend on any one student.[22] When teachers see students for only one hour or so, and no more than five times a week, the capability to build effective teacher-student relationships is severely limited. Knowing students as persons rather than as a line in a grade book cannot occur when the teacher is overwhelmed by the number of students they are assigned. This is especially the case when the teacher is confronted with the challenge of overcoming students' previous negative experiences with teachers.

Self-directedness. Students need to have a sense that they are in charge of their learning, they are responsible for making the important decisions about their work, and they are not simply implementing what the teacher has decided they need to do.[23] Unfortunately, school personnel may assume that teachers or counsellors need to provide more control and direction to put the student on a good path and help keep them on it. Even when this increased control is implemented with the best of intentions, it is to often counterproductive.

Schedule and time flexibility. Factors such as bus schedules and arbitrary decisions about the length of classes, as well as other state or district policies, are often the basis for when and how long a learning experience is permitted to occur. The U.S. Department of Education Commission on Time and Learning spoke to the need to provide more time and schedule flexibility, maintaining that schools needed to make time variable, rather than the learning content.[24] If and when a student fails to accomplish a learning objective, he or she should recognize it was not because the school personnel gave up on them. Put simply: An 8:00 AM to 3:00 PM schedule for school does not mesh with the life situation of many high school students.

Digital media. There are probably more bad examples of digital media being used for students who have been defined as potential dropouts by their school than good ones. Many school personnel seem to think that the student can be given a set of headphones and a computer work station and the device does the rest! While this is not an effective approach, digital media can enable the teacher to become what has been called a "constructive partner" with his or her student.[25] It is this type of relationship that provides a quite different approach to the construction of a learning agenda and implementation of it for the student. When digital media is used well, the student has a resource which is needed for him or her to become an active learner. Another important benefit that digital media provides is that learning need not be confined to a given and set span of time. Digital media provides the means to offer learning anytime, anywhere, which is a critical element in the construction of a learning environment that responds to students' needs and life situations. Thus, digital media becomes an important means of contending with the individual schedules of students. Moreover, digital media can provide a wealth of learning resources that could not have been imagined a relatively short time ago.

We have a good knowledge base for efforts to respond to the need to provide quality learning for young people who have not had a record of success. The six elements described above provide the "best practices" framework for W-A-Y. The "magic ingredient," however, is the people. It is a staff who cultivates an ethos of teacher-student mutual respect and who fosters confidence in the student's capability for success. W-A-Y was created because of the belief that we can and must do better. The manner in which that belief is embodied in the operation of W-A-Y schools is the topic of the next chapter.

THREE

A New Environment for Learning

W-A-Y is based on a fundamental principle: Major change in the organizational culture of the school is necessary to substantially improve the educational life of students whose educational needs were not being met in traditional high schools. As we saw in Chapter One, that principle led Beth Baker and Glen Taylor to establish W-A-Y. Their task was not to renovate schooling, but to reconstruct it.

Students who enter W-A-Y find a learning environment that is quite different from what most of them experienced in their previous schools. This is reflected in different practices, customs, and resources. Of critical importance is the nature of the social environment. W-A-Y students and teachers have restructured roles and interact and relate to one another in a manner not typically seen in typical middle and high schools.

"Widening advancement for youth" is not just a nice-sounding phrase; it is a deeply held commitment of the W-A-Y staff. The goal of W-A-Y is not simply to enable students to acquire a diploma, but to support their acquisition of knowledge, skills, and dispositions that put them on track to live a productive and satisfying life after graduating.

To understand W-A-Y, it is necessary to get past abstractions and clichés and experience the reality of W-A-Y from a student's perspective. Thus, in this chapter we will follow a fictitious student, whom we will call Daryl, from entry into the W-A-Y Program to graduation. By following him, we can get a concrete sense of life as a W-A-Y student. It is important to point out, however, that there is no such thing as a "typical" W-A-Y student—each student brings their own unique personalities, aspirations, learning experiences, strengths, and weaknesses to the Program. (This will be illustrated in the next chapter.) Recognizing the diversity of W-A-Y students, site personnel do not use labels to categorize W-A-Y students as "drop-outs" or "at risk." Labels such as those put the student into a box and make it easier for school personnel to think of them as a type rather than as a unique person. While Daryl is not a real student, information about his experience with W-A-Y is derived from real students.

DISCOVERING W-A-Y

Daryl was having problems in his high school and falling further and further behind in graduation credits. It was becoming increasingly clear to him that he would not graduate. For him, dropping out of school was less like a singular event than the culmination of a process that had been going on for several years. His problems had begun in middle school. Whether it was true or not, he felt that there was no staff person at his high school who cared about him. On the last day of his school year, he walked out of his school without talking to any school staff members. He was certain that he would not return to school, but he had no plan for the next chapter in his life. He considered joining the U.S. Navy, until he discovered that a diploma or GED was required.

In a conversation with a friend, Daryl learned that his friend's brother, Michael, was in a high school program called W-A-Y. Daryl talked with Michael and he had good things to say about the Program. While there was no W-A-Y partner program in Daryl's school district, there was a W-A-Y Academy campus not far from where he lived.

W-A-Y uses a variety of methods to get the word out about their program, such as radio and newspaper advertisements, as well as flyers and brochures that are distributed in places that reach potential students and their parents. Yet, as it was for Daryl, word of mouth is how most students hear about W-A-Y, particularly if their school district is not a partner district.

One of the features of W-A-Y that Michael told Daryl about, and that Daryl found particularly attractive, is that W-A-Y operates on a twelve-month, 24/7 basis. W-A-Y understands that pressures of time and energy often affect high school students negatively. Some students have jobs, children, or other family commitments that distract them from school or conflict with school schedules. Daryl had a part-time job that provided some financial help to his family. With W-A-Y, he could easily make his school work fit around his job schedule. Even though the on-site Academy was not open 24/7, he would be able to continue his school work in the evening, along the on-line help which was always available to him.

Daryl contacted the W-A-Y office by phone and was given a time to meet at the Academy near him. At that time, he would provide the information needed to apply, and to begin his work as a W-A-Y student

THE INDUCTION PROCESS

On a September morning, Daryl walked into the W-A-Y Academy for his induction. There he would receive an orientation about the W-A-Y learning environment and take the first steps in forming relationships with the staff and other students. As he entered, he saw that the environment around him did not look or feel much like a school. Although the room resembled the computer lab at Daryl's previous school, the activity and interaction were definitely not familiar. Unlike what a student encounters in a typical classroom, where the teacher in charge is quite evident, it was not apparent who was in charge as students did their work, moved about the room, talked with one another, or interacted with adults who were in the room. The room had tables and chairs with computers on them. Some students were working with a computer, alone or with one or two other students. In the corner of the room he saw what looked like a teacher with a group of seven or eight students who seemed to be doing school work.

A staff member introduced himself to Daryl and invited him to join five other students who, like him, were there for their induction into W-A-Y. The tone of the induction was relaxed and informal. The person conducting the induction gave Daryl and the other students information on how W-A-Y operates. Background music was playing in the room, and it certainly was not elevator music! Instead, it was instrumental hip-hop that had been selected by the staff person conducting the induction. Snacks were available.

Researchers being inducted into W-A-Y meet in small groups of no more than six, so they are not overwhelmed by meeting a lot of new people. This lets them feel comfortable in conversations with the W-A-Y staff and the other students. Additionally, the personalized music choices and the availability of snacks welcome students into an informal setting. These details may seem trivial, but they are not. From a student's first contact with W-A-Y, an effort is made to create a welcoming atmosphere that tells the researcher: This is a very different school than where you have been in the past. It is important that students entering W-A-Y get the implicit message that this is a student-centered environment.

Daryl and the others with him in his induction received a laptop computer for home use. Three of the students in Daryl's induction group had a computer in their home, but none had their own personal computer. Daryl stayed after the meeting to get additional help in getting his computer set-up. Additionally, he lived in a neighborhood where it would be unsafe to walk back to his Academy with his computer, so he talked to his team leader after the meeting and the team leader agreed to deliver it to his house.

During the induction process Daryl was informed about the various roles of staff members. He learned that there are no personnel on the W-A-Y staff who carry the formal designation of "teacher." W A-Y staff who work with students have specific roles: **mentors, team leaders**, and **content experts**. Similarly, W-A-Y students are not actually called "students." Daryl initially found it weird that the W-A-Y staff called him and the other students "researchers" rather than "students." He did not think of himself as a "researcher." He was just a student! As he eventually got to know more about life inside the W-A-Y community, however, he would realize that calling him a researcher made sense, since his learning occurred because of the research he accomplished on the various topics of his curriculum. He would eventually come to see that he was indeed a researcher.

Mentors are certified teachers who act as learning coaches. The role of the mentor is to build a positive relationship with the researcher and assist them as they proceed through the Program. W-A-Y maintains a low mentor-to-student ratio to personalize the learning environment. W-A-Y does not just "re-brand" teachers as "mentors," simply using a new term for an existing role would be of no value.

The job description of "mentor" details expectations for performance that make it clear that the promise of a student-centered learning experience is more than just empty words:

- Take an active part in the W-A-Y online learning community and assist students with navigating the learning community.
- Uphold the ethos of W-A-Y Program.
- Collaborate with other staff members to assist students through the learning process.
- Guide students in using W-A-Y Program digital media.
- Keep records of students' work and learning plans through weekly reporting.
- Enjoy working with teenagers, so that effective communication can take place.
- Be sympathetic to the problems that have resulted in the disengagement of students from school.
- Enjoy using technology and be enthusiastic about acquiring new information and communications skills.
- Be able to communicate with the students in an informal and friendly way.
- Be persistent and encouraging without being punitive.
- Effectively communicate student learning and support needs to team leaders and other W-A-Y Program staff.

Most school districts do not have an official job description for "teacher." For those that do it would be quite rare for it to contain words such as: "enjoy working with teenagers," "be sympathetic," "be persistent and encouraging," "communicate in an informal and friendly way," or "uphold the ethos" of their school community. The specifics of the job descriptions for W-A-Y personnel close the gap between simply making a claim and building into the Program concrete requirements to implement the claim. That language in the role description does not exist for PR purposes. W-A-Y staff members are expected to display those qualities in their behavior.

Content experts are highly qualified in their endorsement area (eg... math, science, language arts, etc.) and are proficient in the use of digital media for learning. They provide researchers and staff with knowledge of the various disciplines included in the high school curriculum and help researchers make use of HERO, the learning management system that was created by W-A-Y personnel. (More on HERO later in this chapter.) Content experts work with researchers to find learning activities of interest to the researcher that meet graduation credit requirements. They also assist researchers in the accomplishment of the project. Content experts are required to be supportive and share their expertise with mentors to help facilitate student learning.

While researchers in W-A-Y benefit from having staff in the roles described above to assist and support them in their schoolwork, they might get lost in the Program if there was no one person who had the responsibility to supervise every aspect of their life in W-A-Y. That person is the **team leader**. Each researcher is provided with a team leader who is a certified teacher. The team leader oversees all aspects of the researcher's education. Team leaders also assist with the identification of available local resources to support the researcher's learning, such as internships, community projects, and social services. Researchers meet with team leaders at the W-A-Y sites and can also contact the team leader by phone or receive one-on-one instructional support in person at the W-A-Y lab. Additionally, the W-A-Y network makes possible communication and interaction between researchers and the W-A-Y staff using email, posting, discussion boards, instant messaging, and video conferencing.

Some of the responsibilities specified in the official job description of team leaders are:

- Assist young people in removing barriers to learning by collaborating across networks.
- Communicate with the W-A-Y central team to ensure that the W-A-Y Program model, policy and practice is followed.

- Monitor project deliverables and communications to ensure follow-up and continuity between mentors and researchers.
- Monitor mentor reports and other such requirements.
- Ensure that child protection issues are dealt with promptly, keeping the local project team informed.
- Ensure that no student is offline for technical reasons for more than 48 hours.
- Ensure that each student has access to the standard equipment and connectivity.
- Ensure that student progress data required by W-A-Y Program central team is accurate and up to date.

For W-A-Y to be successful, the administrators must find individuals who can work in an environment that is unlike the traditional high school. New persons coming onto the staff must have a disposition that aligns with the W-A-Y culture. Teachers who see themselves as the focal point of the learning environment do not fare well as W-A-Y staff members. While it is not difficult to provide training to personnel pertaining to W-A-Y procedures such as using the W-A-Y computer system, the methods for assessing researcher performance, the filing of researcher records and other data, it is difficult or impossible to train someone to embody the attitudes and dispositions that are expected for W-A-Y personnel if they do not already exhibit these. Finding and employing the right personnel is critical to enabling W-A-Y to make what it promises a reality.

Position openings are posted on a wide variety of sites that reach teachers and other school personnel. Those applying are screened by the school site director (principal), and a list of those who will be invited to the first interview is developed. All teachers who are being considered for a position must be Michigan-certified in their content area. Those doing the screening pay particular attention to teachers with experience, particularly when they have worked with students similar to those in W-A-Y.

The interviewers for the first round of interviews for prospective staff members consist of the school site director and at least one other staff member. Some applicants are invited to a second-round interview with the director and at least two other staff members. Some sites include researchers in the interview process. Following conversation among the interviewees, one of the applicants is invited to join the staff, and a date for their three-day training session is chosen so that it will occur within their first ten days of employment.

When new staff members begin their work, they spend several days observing the "real life" operation of W-A-Y, and they receive coaching and mentoring from staff members. W-A-Y site administrators understand that the role of a staff member in the Program is quite different from what a teacher might have experienced in previsions work as a teacher job or administrator in a traditional school or what they learned in their teacher education program. A good portion of the three-day training for a new staff member pertains to project based learning (PBL), which is the main method for delivering the curriculum to W-A-Y researchers. (More information will be provided on PBL later in this chapter.) Additional training specific to PBL is also provided when such is needed. For example, in the 2017/2018 the administration saw a need for some "refresher training" pertaining to the use of the W-A-Y project based learning system, so, there was an additional three-day training session on PBL.

Staff members get one day of professional development per month. Also, there are professional development sessions on specific issues or topics. Central administrators keep an eye on researcher data and respond with professional development when a need becomes evident. For example, in the 2017/2018 year, some staff members expressed concerns about researcher writing. As a result, a three-day professional development session on writing was held for staff. Also, in the current year there was an additional five-day professional development session for team leaders and site administrators.

Professional development in W-A-Y is not just a "top down" matter. There is recognition that staff members have their own development needs, which go beyond the professional development provided for the entire staff, so they are given the opportunity to attend workshops when the staff member believes they can help them improve their capabilities. Since W-A-Y staffs are not in standalone classrooms, it is less disruptive for them to attend workshops or specialized training.

After learning about staff roles at W-A-Y and their own roles as researchers rather than students, inductees receive their own laptops. Researchers need varying degrees of help setting up their computer, and of course, they all need specific guidance on using the W-A-Y computer and Internet resources. In some instances, staff delay giving the researcher their computer and encourage them to come to the site so that staff can provide additional support in getting them comfortable with the use of the device and the W-A-Y data systems.

Researchers are given an AirCard to enable them to connect to the Internet from their home and to access the W-A-Y server. The computers provided for researcher use are compliant with the Federal Children's Internet Protection Act, which requires schools to filter objectionable material for researchers. While W-A-Y recognizes that others in the researcher's home may use the computer, the researcher and parents are informed that their researcher has priority use of the device and needs to have access to it whenever he or she needs to use it. Theft or breakage of computers has not been a problem.

The induction process generally lasts from two to three hours, but some researchers will stay longer because they have additional questions or concerns. Also, some researchers may want to get additional information or may wish to ask questions they did not ask during the formal induction meeting because they forgot to ask them or preferred to ask in private, as when Daryl expressed concerns about walking home with his computer. Some parents come with their sons or daughters to the induction process, and when they do W-A-Y staff provides them with an orientation to the Program. Several W-A-Y sites hold a session for parents concurrent with the researcher induction. W-A-Y staff members create linkages with parents or parent surrogates. Parents are shown how they can log into the W-A-Y researcher information system to check their researcher's progress. In addition to involving parents in the induction process, W-A-Y staff frequently make home visits.

Daryl left the induction with lots of information and recognition that what he had experienced in the three hours at the W-A-Y Academy was quite different from what school was in his mind. He was not yet convinced he had made the right decision; he realized that all of what he had heard could have just been a good sales pitch. Yet, he left the W-A-Y site feeling maybe – just maybe – he had come to the right place.

MICHIGAN MERIT CURRICULUM

High school graduation requirements for Michigan students are contained in the Michigan Merit Curriculum.[1] As of September 2017, at least 18 credits are required for graduation in the following content areas: four credits of English language arts; four credits of math; three credits of social science; three credits of science; one credit of visual, performing or applied art; one credit of physical education; and two credits of a world language. All schools in Michigan require several electives for graduation, so the required number of credits for graduation always exceeds 18. Twenty-two credits are required for graduation from a W-A-Y Academy. The credits required for graduation from a partner school district vary from district to district but are close to what W-A-Y Academies require.

The Michigan Merit Curriculum goes beyond requiring specific courses for graduation; it details the specific standards that need to be achieved in the various content areas. For example, three of the standards for the earth science course are:

> Describe natural processes in which heat transfer in the earth occurs by conduction, convection, and radiation.
>
> Describe geologic, paleontologic, and paleoclimatalogic evidence that indicates Africa and South America were once part of a single continent.
>
> Describe relative humidity in terms of the moisture content of the air and the moisture capacity of the air and how these depend on the temperature.[2]

Those standards illustrate the specificity of Michigan high school graduation requirments.

School districts certify that the courses in their high school curriculum meet the curriculum standards for the various subjects. The student receives a grade for the course, but there is no break-down pertaining to each of the standards contained in the course. W-A-Y goes a big step beyond this approach and lists the standareds required for gaining credit for each required course. The researcher's accomplishment of the course is a reult of good performance on each of the standards that comprise the course.

DARYL'S LEARNING PLAN

The first step in moving forward with Daryl's education at W-A-Y was an audit of his transcript from his previous school. The audit was done by his team leader to find out which graduation requirements he had met and those he had yet to accomplish. Even though Daryl had been at his previous school for two years he had only achieved five credits. A high school student who was on track for graduation from a W-A-Y Academy in four years would have gained five or six credits when they are beginning their sophomore year. Thus, Daryl was about a year behind the class with which he began his high school education.

Daryl needed seventeen more credits in the required content areas for graduation. He worked with his team leader to develop his learning plan. The learning plan is the researchers "road map" with regard to successful attainment of their diploma. The conversation about the learning plan between Daryl and his team leader helped his team leader gain insights into Daryl's preferences and aversions that would be reflected in suggestions by him and other W-A-Y staff in implementing his learning plan.

Researchers become very knowledgeable about the standards they need to meet in order accomplish the course. As they continue in the Program, their learning plan shows their progress toward graduation as well as a projected graduation date based on the rate they are progressing. A researcher may wish to graduate sooner than the projected date, which can be accomplished by that researcher increasing their pace of learning. Sometimes an event or development in the researcher's life causes them to slow down their work. In either case, the W-A-Y Program can accommodate the situation. The point is that the researcher is in the "driver's seat" with regard to the pace of their progress and is intimately familiar with the standards they are expected to meet to graduate.

THE W-A-Y LEARNING COMMUNITY

It is easy for anyone who would have met with Daryl and the others with him to recognize that each of those young people were individuals with different life stories, interests, aptitudes, and goals. There is, however, one perspective that most of the young people who enter W-A-Y share: School has not been a good experience. They do not leave behind their negative beliefs and opinions of school when they walk in the door at a W-A-Y site. W-A-Y staff members have learned to "take this in stride" and to be mindful of the fact that this negative perspective will change over time as the young person recognizes that this is really a quite different type of school.

The W-A-Y experience is a fresh start, but it is by no means a free pass! Researchers will see that the staff holds them to high expectations. As W-A-Y researchers they are not immune from some aspects of learning that are endemic to the process. They will be challenged. They will run into difficulties. They will struggle with learning tasks that seem impenetrable. Yet, they will increasingly come to understand that the human and technical resources of W-A-Y can enable them to succeed. There is a qualitative difference between doing hard work where the person believes in their ability to ultimately succeed in contrast to hard work where the person believes that failure is the most likely consequence.

In Daryl's previous school, the instructional method had been mainly based on learning the material in the text book, as well as that presented by the teacher in the classroom. There was some use of small group learning, but that was done to supplement the textbook and the teacher. The pace of the learning was determined by the teacher's lesson plans. Teachers could give some individual attention to a student who was struggling were they so disposed, but time constraints had generally put a tight limit on how much individual attention the teacher, and even very good teachers, could provide. At W-A-Y, Daryl discovered that he had as much or as little time as he needed to be successful with his learning objectives. Daryl's team leader monitored his progress and, if Daryl experienced a lack of progress as a consequence of not working on the project in question, the team leader intervened to see if he could help get Daryl back on task.

Removal of the time constraint and overcrowding common to so many American public schools is a critical element in the W-A-Y approach. Maintaining a low ratio of researchers to teachers is essential to create the type of learning environment that W-A-Y seeks to create. The staff's interaction with researchers sends a clear message to the young people in the Program: we are here to work with you, support you, and accept you for who you are. Researchers have immediate access to staff who can help them overcome learning difficulties. It is terribly difficult to do this when a teacher has more students than time.

PROJECT BASED LEARNING AND THE W-A-Y LEARNING MANAGEMENT SYSTEM

W-A- Y understands that the critical task in education is to make the learning align with the person rather than attempting to align the person with the curriculum. In other words, personalized learning is at the heart of W-A-Y. It has become common practice for school districts to assert that "personalized learning" is current practice. Statements such as the one below are widely prevalent in school districts' descriptions of district philosophy:

> The School District of X shares in the vision of excellence through personalized learning, an approach to learning and instruction that is designed around individual learner readiness, needs, strengths and interests. Learners are active participants in setting goals, planning learning paths, tracking progress and determining how learning will be demonstrated. Through a personalized approach that recognizes unique learning differences and preferences in students, we work to meaningfully engage all learners focusing on communication, critical thinking, collaboration, and creativity.[3]

It may be the case that the school district quoted above is, in fact, implementing practices that do in fact personalize learning; however, frequently the basis for the claim is not evident in school practices. School district personnel are not necessarily being deceitful when they contend that they are personalizing instruction. For many schools, personalizing learning is more of an aspiration than a reality. Many policies and practices that are locked into school districts present difficult obstacles to achieve the goal of personalized learning. The success that W-A-Y has had working with researchers who have previously not fared well in school is because W-A-Y staff treat the personalization of learning not as a slogan but as a—if not *the*—critical aspect of the teaching/learning environment.

As has been stated, project based learning (PBL) is at the heart of the learning approach used by W-A-Y to connect the curriculum to each individual researcher, and it is a critical element in the W-A-Y approach to personalizing learning. PBL involves a theme focus, often interdisciplinary, and engages students in research, learning, and problem solving around that theme. Students demonstrate their competency of the various learning objectives of the project, not with a score on a test, but with the accomplishment of the project.

In the typical high school, students may encounter PBL at some point in their high school courses, but it typically will not be a dominant learning approach that the student will experience. For W-A-Y, project based learning is not a garnish. It is the entrée! The critical question is: To what extent and in what ways does the unique nature of each researcher actually affect the nature and implementation of their education in their school?

Peter Glen has been deeply involved in the development and use of project based learning, one of the "hottest buzzwords in education."[4] Nevertheless, he reports that only 1% of schools use it. It is difficult to validate his statistic, but PBL is far from mainstream in most schools. PBL is the key that unlocks schools' capability to make the curriculum content fit individual students, creates an active and engaging learning environment for students, and is also rewarding for teachers. Ryan Steuer, Executive Director at Magnify Learning, a network that offers professional development for PBL to schools and districts, put it this way: "The truth about PBL is, that once you learn the skills, culture and best practices, you find you are teaching the way you always dreamed you would."[5]

In discussing what could be done to make PBL more widely used, Glen makes several recommendations. The first recommendation is that there needs to be an organizational "community of interest" so that the teacher is not isolated as they implement PBL. No teacher working alone can provide the large number of projects needed to accommodate a wide array of topics that can engage the student. Second, it is important that teachers get the training they need to make best practice use of PBL. Finally, there is need for a "plug and play" resource for teachers. If the teacher were required to create every project from "scratch," the task would be overwhelming. All of Glen's recommendations are embodied in the use of PBL by W-A-Y.

DARYL MEETS HERO

HERO is the learning management system used by W-A-Y to guide learners to projects and resources that best fit their unique interests, goals, and learning styles. Projects that blend standards with real world applications, crossing disciplines, developing the problem-solving skills that both adult and youth learners need. HERO develops in students a love of learning and exploration to last a lifetime. Researchers can create their own project, select from those from those available in HERO, or modify a project in HERO to enable them to make it a better fit for them. When researchers modify a project, they can then see which standards they are meeting and what more needs to be done to accomplish a course that is required by the Michigan Merit Curriculum. It is quite common that the content expert will modify the project to make a better fit with the researcher. The projects in HERO contain issues, topics, and problems which must be created or solved, and blend standards with real world applications. Most projects are cross-disciplinary, so that in completing the project the researcher will earn credits in more than one area. As an example, a researcher may choose a project that involves reading for meaning, with the material being read pertaining to social studies. If the researcher is successful with that project they will be building credits for both the English language arts and social studies courses.

As he began his schooling at W-A-Y, Daryl was not left to his own devices to find projects for the standards he had to accomplish. He received assistance from the staff to find a project that appealed to him and that would meet several of the standards he needed to accomplish. He looked through the projects available in HERO, W-A-Y's learning management system, and selected one called "Limitless." The project was about choosing a new cell phone, which appealed to him because he was actually interested in doing that himself. Beyond just doing Google searches for phones, the project required Daryl to produce a tangible product: a presentation to community members explaining which cell phone plan would be best for them and their needs. This project met standards in algebra 1 and technology.

First, Daryl viewed a video that launched the project. After watching the video, he got into the project he had selected. Four screenshots are presented below to give some concrete sense of what projects in the HERO system look like. Figure 1 shows the project's driving question and entry event. The key question is: "How do I decide which cell phone is best?"

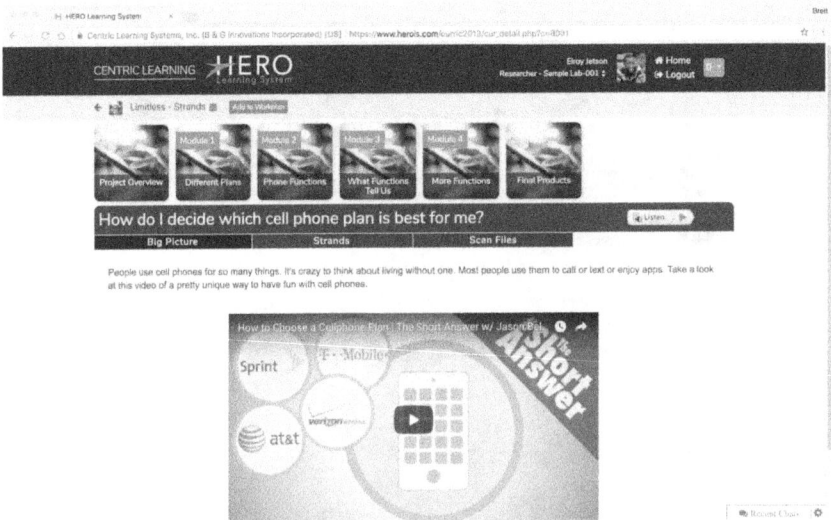

Figure 1: Screenshot of the driving question and
entry event to the "Limitless" project.

Daryl saw how this project aligned with national and state standards. He also saw the evaluation rubrics for each of the standards this project could meet. Each of the projects is assessed for mastery of the content area standards utilizing a proficiency-based rubric which describes the levels of proficiency for each standard.

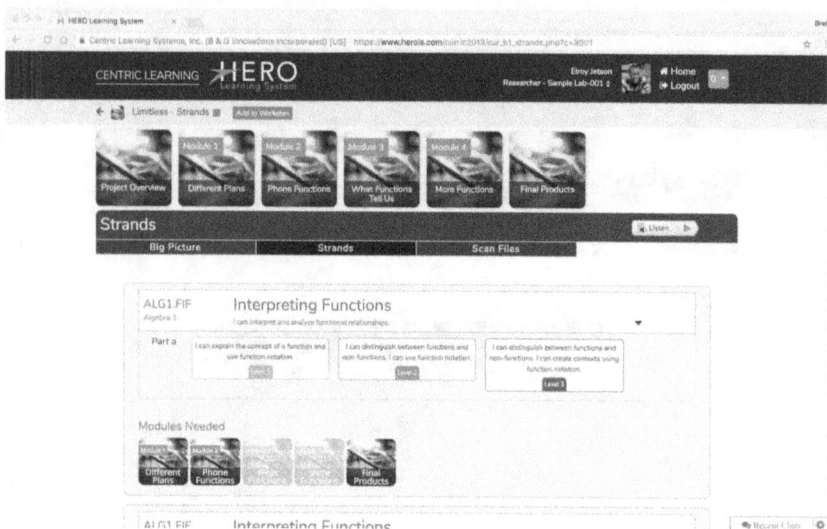

Figure 2: Screenshot of the national and state standards and proficiency-based rubric of "Limitless" project.

Daryl then saw the online instruction of the project. The online instruction included digital content, resources, and tools to be used as he worked on the project. Daryl could move through the instruction at his own pace, have flexible physical attendance, and get individualized instruction as needed from a W-A-Y staff member. The content expert working with him could modify the instruction and learning experience to be compatible with Daryl's needs and interests. This setup made it clear to Daryl what was expected of him but provided him control over his learning. He had the freedom to set his own pace and decide how to demonstrate what was expected of him.

While Daryl worked on this project, his math content expert saw that he was having some problems with the math, so he arranged for Daryl and four other researchers who seemed to be having similar problems to join a small learning group that was meeting in the lab.

Figure 3: Description of Figure 3 here.

Screenshot four shows the culminating activity of the Limitless Project. At the end of the project, Daryl had to give a presentation to a public audience that presented his findings on which cell phone plan was best. This public product raised the stakes for Daryl's work and lead to higher quality work than he had been producing in his previous high school. It also demonstrated to Daryl that the work he did on this project was valuable to those outside the classroom.

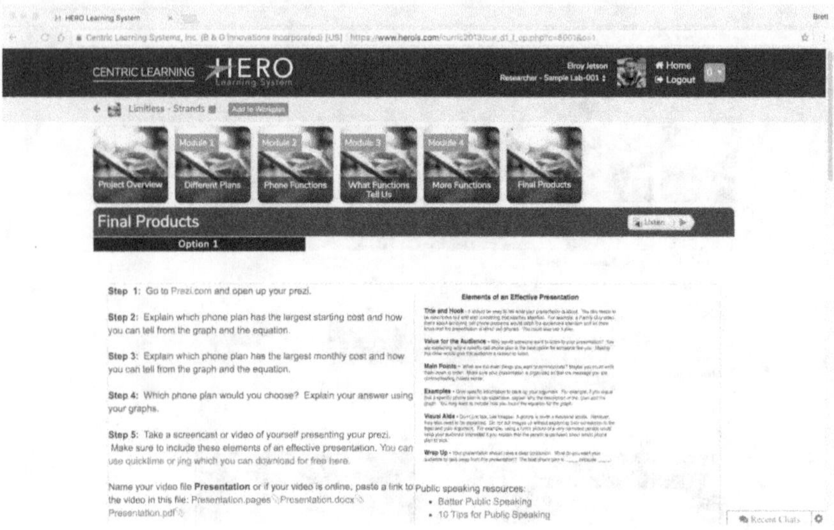

Figure 4: The culminating activity of "Limitless" project.

Limitless is only one of the projects available to W-A-Y researchers. Three others are:

How To

In this project, students create an instructional video to teach other students a technology skill. Their video is hosted in the online support area for other students to use. In the process, students learn how to use technology tools, organize knowledge, and present content to an audience.

Dream an Invention

In this project, students identify a problem in the world that they would like to fix. Students create a solution to this problem by using the design thinking process to build an invention. In the process, students create a business proposal for their invention in hope to secure an investor and submit a patent for it.

Protect the Strays

In this project, students will take on the role as an owner of a company that creates warming packs. This company has been approached by the ASPCA who are looking to hire students to create warming packs for their winter shelter bins. The shelter bins are for their stray cats throughout the state of Michigan.

In 2018, at the time of this writing, there were approximately 9000 projects in HERO, but this number is continuously expanding. Projects are created by the W-A-Y central staff and by content experts both on-line and at sites. A researcher may also work with a content expert to create a project from scratch. For example, an online researcher who is a serious dance student co-created with her W-A-Y content expert a project on dance which could meet some of her physical education requirements.

Projects have also emerged from specialized activities. For example, a private company was hired to offer a six-week program in physics, which involved some on-site activities and a field trip. As a result of this program, researchers developed a project involving a roller coaster that applied physics knowledge they had acquired. They had produced various materials that were incorporated into a project on the design of roller coasters; this project is now contained within HERO as an option for other researchers.

As Daryl completed projects and proceeded through the Program, it became quite clear to him that his decisions were key in shaping his educational experience. Earlier in the Program he wished from time to time that someone would just tell him what to do rather than putting this burden on him, but as he became more acclimated to how things were done in W-A-Y he felt better and better about being in charge of his education.

RESEARCHER ASSESSMENT AND PROGRAM MONITORING

As Daryl completed projects, his work and production were viewed by members of staff. He was also followed closely within the reporting system to ensure that he received any necessary social or academic interventions in a timely manner. His team leader and mentor submitted weekly reports for review by the Program directors. While Daryl had left his previous school without much notice from school personnel, such an event was quite unlikely to happen at W-A-Y.

On one language arts project, Daryl received a score of "P," or "provisional," which meant that he would not receive course credit for that project in its current form. At that point, the feedback from the content expert he was working with became an important asset for him. He was told exactly what was needed to improve his project. After some conversation, Daryl came to understand what needed to be fixed. So indeed, there was more work to do; Daryl knew exactly what was needed, and upon re-submission he received a score of "2" out of 3 and course credit.

Team leaders, mentors, and content experts all pay close attention to researcher progress and products. If a researcher is not participating, such will be visible to the staff and administration. While it does happen that a researcher leaves the program, it is not possible for a researcher who is in the Program to be in a non-participating status. In such an instance, a staff member will intervene to see what can be done to remediate the situation. In traditional schools, students receive a grade on work that has been submitted, but that grade does not provide information about what the student would need to do to improve the project, since that is generally not an option. W-A-Y uses a 3-point grading system, with "3" being the highest score. Researchers receive a "P," or a "provisional," if the project in its current form would not receive course credit. In conventional school settings, the student would probably receive a grade of "F," which means that he or she has failed. As we saw with Daryl's experience, a grade of "P" indicates that the researcher has not met the learning goal of a particular project; however, it keeps the door open for the researcher to make improvements and to re-submit his or her project for assessment.

Content experts are responsible for assessments of researcher projects. In order for assessments to be credible there must be consistency of ratings among different raters. This is accomplished by bringing together the content experts in groups pertaining to their field of expertise and engaging them in collective review of the rubrics used for researcher evaluation by examining them and isolating key words in the rubrics. This provides the basis for conversations to sharpen the language of the evaluation rubrics and to come to an agreement on the definitions of terms. The content experts then assess a project they have never seen before and determine whether there is sufficient inter-rater reliability with that rubric, or if more scrutiny and conversation is needed. There is one other check for the assessment process: W-A-Y administrators can see how their colleagues are rating projects and raise a "red flag" when it becomes evident that a content expert is either overly lenient or overly stringent in their assessments.

HERO maintains information about all aspects of the researchers' learning activities and progress. The monitoring system also enables the administration to assess the progress of the researchers they are serving as a group and to respond to any problematic situations. The information in HERO makes it possible for the researcher or a staff member to monitor researcher progress on a monthly, weekly, or even daily basis. The HERO system contains information on the projects the researcher is working on, the standards—and scores—of the projects they have accomplished, the standards that need to be achieved to graduate, and the time spent online and in the lab. All of this information is available to the researcher and staff. The site director can also assess how promptly researchers are receiving feedback. Thus, the door is always open for continuous improvement of work being done by a researcher.

THE DAY THAT MIGHT NEVER HAVE COME

On a June day two years after Daryl entered W-A-Y, Daryl and his mother went to the lab to attend his graduation ceremony. There was a joyous atmosphere in the room, not only with the graduates, but also with the family members and friends in attendance. The superintendent and the site director gave short speeches. As is always the case, the most moving aspect of the graduation ceremony was a speech by the valedictorian.

What follows is the unedited valedictorian speech from one of the 2017 W-A-Y graduations.

> Welcome, humans. Last week I found out that I had to write a speech for graduation. Here I am in front of you, while my organs are dancing with each other. So let's begin.

> My name is Alondra Cruz aka Alondra The Majestic and I want to talk about failure...not the best topic for a graduation but I wasn't the best option to write this speech. Everyone knows that I love Doctor Who. If you didn't, now you know. Because of this love, I will explain a quote from the show.

In the episode "Vincent and the Doctor"(This is me citing my source BTW), the Doctor says "The way I see it, every life is a pile of good things and bad things. The good things don't always soften the bad things, but vice-versa, the bad things don't always spoil the good things and make them unimportant." I wanted to share this quote with you because today everyone is going to talk about the success you will have in life. Let's keep it real, we won't all succeed at everything we do, and when we do, it may not be on our first try. It's a good thing to be optimistic, but remember life is not a fairy tale. We are going to face this enemy called failure more than once in our future, but that's life. The important part is what are you going to do when you fail? I am not here to tell you what you should do. Do whatever you want, except illegal stuff.

The meaning of this quote is that it is okay to fail and feel bad but don't let your failure ruin your success. Don't let a bad day ruin you. Because at least once in our lifetime we have felt like Vincent Van Gogh felt all his life.

He felt alone and misunderstood. He never got to see his awesomeness in his life. He died believing he was a failure and his art was worth nothing. Everyone knows who Van Gogh was and what he represents in art. Maybe you feel like a failure. That's not true, you have value. Everyone is important in their unique way and that's the beauty of life.

Not so long ago high school graduation had seemed as remote to Daryl as a trip to the moon. At that point in his life, as he looked to the future, he had had little reason for optimism. A couple of months before his graduation, he had met with an advisor at a local community college and explored a field of interest to him: emergency medical technician. His meeting with the advisor confirmed his sense that this was the direction for his career. He spoke with his W-A-Y mentor, who helped him get his transcript to the college. Certainly, Daryl was likely to face new challenges as he moved forward with his life. But his optimism was warranted.

AND, IN CONCLUSION....

W-A-Y exists in the real world. As such, it is not immune to national, state, and local politics. The founders of W-A-Y put the Program within the sphere of public education. Certainly, to have created W-A-Y as a private school would have provided much greater autonomy. Yet, their goal in creating W-A-Y was not to destroy public education, but to change it.

Most people become teachers because they sincerely want to help young people learn and flourish. Unfortunately, too often they find themselves in a situation where the best they can do is hindered or prohibited by the rules, customs, and practices of the schools where they work. In essence, W-A-Y provides an environment where school personnel have few impediments to doing what is right for the young people they are there to help. Not all teachers, administrators, parents, or politicians would feel comfortable with W-A-Y. For some, it moves too far from their beliefs about how teaching and learning has operated and should operate. Yet, for those educators who join the W-A-Y community, it is exactly where they want to be!

The W-A-Y academies provide fewer constraints on school practices and policies, but the partner schools involve working with school districts who understand what W-A-Y is and how it operates and who have invited W-A-Y into the district. Providing an opportunity for teachers and administrators to actually function in a different environment is more effective than persuasion or admonishment in helping them to feel confident about the change they are fostering. The experts in the effect W-A-Y is having on those young people in the Program are the young people themselves and those in the various teaching roles. As such, the teachers who staff the partner sites and who are district employees are acquiring experience in a quite different learning environment. The most powerful evidence one can see about W-A-Y's achievements comes from direct contact with the young people and the staff at the various W-A-Y sites. The next chapter will give some snapshots of researchers and staff members. As the reader will see, each person has a story to tell and the stories of the researchers play a highly significant role in motivating the staff to not let them down.

FOUR

Listening to the Voices of Researchers and Staff Members

The best approach to understanding W-A-Y is to walk into a W-A-Y school, observe what is happening, and talk to researchers and staff members. Since that is impractical or impossible for most readers of this book, this chapter will provide an approximation of what a person might experience if he or she walked into a W-A-Y site, learned something about the stories of the researchers and staff members who were there, and talked with some of them about illustrative profiles of W-A-Y researchers, along with "snapshots" from conversations with several of them. Thus, the reader of this chapter will have the opportunity to hear about some W-A-Y researchers and hear from others. We will also meet some staff members who will share their opinions about working in W-A-Y. First, however, we will review a survey of W-A-Y researchers and staff conducted in 2015 that provides context for what researchers and staff will tell us about the W-A-Y experience.

RESEARCHER AND STAFF SURVEY

In 2015, surveys were sent to 1,350 researchers, and 689 (51%) were returned. Surveys were also sent to 245 staff; 158 were returned (68%). All responses from staff personnel and researchers were anonymous.

W-A-Y is the acronym for Widening Advancement for Youth. So, the fundamental question in this chapter is this: Did the W-A-Y experience change the participating young people's opinions and beliefs about what they could accomplish in life? It is important to keep in mind that most of the young people in W-A-Y came to it after experiences in schools that had substantially more impact in lowering their expectations for life after school than in raising them.

Two-thirds (67%) of the researchers indicated that W-A-Y had changed their sense of what they could accomplish. Another question pertained to whether they expected to graduate from high school. Of the 689 respondents, 81% of researchers responded "absolutely," 12% replied "probably," and five percent replied "maybe." Only two percent responded, "not likely". No is data available pertaining to how those researchers would have answered this question prior to their involvement with W-A-Y, but since most of the young people who enter W-A-Y do so because they have lost confidence in what they could achieve in the school they were attending, there can be little doubt that substantially fewer of them expected to achieve a high school diploma prior to entering W-A-Y.

As a follow-up to the question about the likelihood of graduating from high school, researchers were asked to reflect on their future after graduation. Over half of the respondents (63%) reported that they were now planning on going to a community college or a four-year university after high school. An additional five percent indicated that they were planning to enter a private technical school after graduation, and 22% reported that they did not have any plans for getting more education after graduation from high school.

Researchers were asked to rank several features of W-A-Y, from those they considered most important aspects of the Program to those they considered least important. The top ranked item was: "Being in an environment that doesn't feel like school used to feel." This was a very important finding for W-A-Y leaders, since the critical quality that Beth and Glen had thought about while designing W-A-Y was that of a learning environment that was markedly different from what they previously experienced.

Other questions were included to explore other issues in the operation of W-A-Y. One of those questions asked if the respondents would recommend W-A-Y to a friend. A majority of researchers (66%) reported that they had already done so; another 21% indicated they would, but had not done so yet; 6% said they did not know if they would do so; and 7% said they would not recommend W-A-Y to a friend. Finally, the questionnaire asked the researchers to rate W-A-Y on a 5 point scale, with 5 as the strongest positive score and 1 as the most negative score. Sixty percent rated their W-A-Y experience at the top two positive scores, and 6% rated it at the bottom two levels of the five-point scale. The others indicated that W-A-Y met their expectations.

SEVEN PROFILES OF W-A-Y RESEARCHERS

Who are the young people relying on W-A-Y to help them move toward a better future? The following profiles that follow are not intended to describe the "typical" researcher in the Program since W-A-Y operates on the premise that there is no "typical" student; rather, they illustrate the diversity of the young people who are members of the W-A-Y community.

Jason: Contending with an Unstable Life Situation

Jason is an 18-year-old researcher who lives with his guardian. He enrolled in W-A-Y with a total of eight high school credits. He transferred to W-A-Y after having attended multiple high schools. Those working with him have been struck by his resilience in the face of the frequent changes he experienced in his academic life and also disruption in his personal life as a result of having had multiple different guardians prior to and while he has been enrolled at W-A-Y.

The flexibility that W-A-Y offers has played a major role in Jason's success in the Program. Since W-A-Y enables him to work at his own pace from home as well as in the lab, he has been able to make up work quickly that he missed because of personal issues and guardianship changes. Jason has benefited from the mentoring he has received. In the past, it was rare for him to be encouraged by the adults in his life. Now there are staff at W-A-Y who express confidence that he can reach his fullest academic potential.

Since enrolling at W-A-Y Jason has earned 16 credits, well above the program's credit goal for a two-year time period. He has consistently met the program requirements for project submission, credit attainment, and lab attendance. Jason has shown growth not only academically, but as a person. It is evident that his confidence in school and life has improved over the last two years as he has established consistency in both areas. He has also increased his GPA to a 3.54. He plans to move out of state after completing his graduation requirements. Currently, he is undecided about what college he would like to attend, but he has completed his FAFSA (Free Application for Federal Student Aid) and intends to apply to several colleges.

Jason has improved in all aspects of his life during his time at W-A-Y. His problems at his previous school were a consequence of the disconnect between the structure of the school and the needs and circumstances of his own life. The W-A-Y Academy he attends has encouraged him to try new things and explore career interests. The W-A-Y staff has commented that working with him was a joy and say that they will miss him after his graduation. They are encouraged knowing he is prepared to have a successful life.

Corrine: Gaining Personal Discipline

Corrine is a 17-year-old researcher who lives with her large family. She enrolled in W-A-Y with a total of 3.25 high school credits. Corrine's younger sister and brother subsequently enrolled in W-A-Y as well. When Corrine entered W-A-Y she struggled to meet her project submission and credit attainment goals. After careful monitoring and multiple conversations with her mentor and team leader, it was clear to her that the biggest factor preventing her from being successful was the amount of time she was spending in the lab talking with others as a means of avoiding her work. As we saw in Chapter One, researchers are free to talk with others in the lab, but staff intervenes when conversation and socializing are excessive and are proving to be a factor in seriously hindering the researchers' progress. Daily interaction with her mentor played a key role in keeping Corrine on track academically. Maturity has also played a major role in her success in the program. She has grown from a 14-year-old child into a young adult who wants to be a role model for her younger siblings, who attend the program with her on a daily basis.

Corrine's response to her mentor, when it has been necessary for her to intervene, is to acknowledge that her mentor is helping her and not just being a nasty teacher. Constant reminders of her goals and conversations around current behaviors are key strategies in ensuring the continuation of her success at W-A-Y. As a result, Corrine's academic performance has improved greatly. At the time of this writing, she has 18.25 high school credits and should be on track to graduate before the end of the summer of 2017. She consistently meets her weekly project submission and credit attainment goals and has completed her FAFSA application. She plans to begin her post-secondary education at Mott Community College.

Maria: Farcing Challenges in a New Country

Maria is a 16-year-old researcher from Central America who lives with her father and stepmother. When Maria entered W-A-Y she was not sure how successful she would be, but now she says, "I feel 100% certain that I will graduate. That is my goal." She came to the U.S. with her father because it was his goal to enable her to get a good education and to go to college, which was not available to her in their country. "He told me he wanted to civilize me," Maria says. Maria does not speak, read, or write English fluently. She first enrolled in W-A-Y in 2016 with no high school credits. The biggest factor thwarting her academic success is her difficulty with English. W-A-Y provided her with a translator who gives her on-going help. She also gets help from other W-A-Y researchers in the lab. She comes to the lab every day, and has missed only three days since she enrolled in W-A-Y.

Maria is self-motivated to learn more and more every day, and she has made progress in overcoming her shyness, which was largely a consequence of her difficulty with English. She is working hard to learn English, so she can graduate and go on to college. Her biggest improvement is that she is more open to starting a conversation with teachers and other researchers and she is not as reluctant when she tries to pronounce new words. She constantly challenges herself to get out of her comfort zone to prove that she can graduate from high school in a country quite unlike her own. Her dedicated work is producing very positive results.

Robert: Medical Problems Hindering School Work

Robert is a 16-year-old transgender researcher who lives with his mother, father, and sister (who is also a researcher at W-A-Y). He had previously been enrolled at an online school, but due to issues with his physical and mental health, he was not successful in that program. Robert has a condition that causes dizziness, as well as a diagnosis of ADHD, anxiety disorder, and depression. Attending school in a traditional environment became too difficult for him due to frequent absences caused by illness and doctor appointments. Even at the online school he previously attended, he felt as if he could never catch up. Before enrolling at W-A-Y, he felt "defeated" and "stupid." Shortly after enrolling at W-A-Y, Robert went through a week-long series of medical tests at the Mayo Clinic in Minnesota for autonomic dysfunction, resulting in a lengthy absence from school.

The flexibility of the W-A-Y schedule allows Robert's family to schedule doctor appointments more easily without absences counting against him. Access to his school work from home using the W-A-Y computer system also makes it possible for him to do his school work when he is too ill to attend school. The accommodating format of the school helps him to not feel overwhelmed even when he has extended absences. He is always able to make up assignments and he starts and finishes projects at his own pace. Robert also benefits from having a mentor and teaching staff that actively encourage him, expressing high expectations. His progress is monitored daily and weekly. Goals and feedback are presented in positive manner.

Since enrolling at W-A-Y two years ago, Robert has earned nearly eight credits. Although he has not consistently met his credit goal, he is now in an age-appropriate grade as a 16-year-old sophomore. On the spring 2015 school district assessment, he scored at an 11th grade level in reading, but only a 4th grade level in math. On the Fall 2016 district assessment, however, he scored at a college level in reading and an 8th grade level in math. He has also demonstrated growth socially and has an increased interest in school activities as demonstrated by his active participation on the school's robotics team. He looks forward to continued participation on the team during his junior and senior years. He hopes that robotics will provide scholarship opportunities.

Robert has also dramatically improved in his emotional response to school. Prior to attending W-A-Y, his school-related anxiety resulted in physical symptoms that prevented attendance. Now he tells the staff that, while he continues to have generalized anxiety, he has no anxiety related directly to the school. He says he feels hopeful, whereas before he did not think he could graduate from high school. He has become an eager researcher with a 3.65 GPA and college aspirations. Robert believes that attending his W-A-Y Academy has provided him with hope and confidence.

Michael: Self-defeating Behaviors

Michael is a 19-year-old researcher who lives with his grandmother. He has experienced many difficult situations throughout his childhood, including watching the violent death of his older brother when he was only five or six years old. When enrolling in W-A-Y in 2015 with a total of seven credits, he was extremely argumentative, struggled academically, and had a difficult time interacting with other researchers and experts in the lab. He was suspended multiple times for making inappropriate comments towards other researchers or staff, causing disruptions in the lab.

Several conferences were held with him and his grandmother to improve his behavior and academic performance. During the course of various conferences, a behavior plan was implemented to improve his lab behavior and social skills. Over time the number of behavioral referrals and suspensions decreased. A plan was also implemented for Robert to meet with his mentor each time he attends lab prior to beginning his work to ensure he is on track with his learning plan, working towards graduation.

The staff's goal for Michael was not only to improve his achievement, but also to develop his self-confidence. Besides meeting with his mentor each time he came to the lab, he also met with his team leader to discuss a strict work plan, which included focusing on only two or three courses at a time to keep him focused and engaged. Michael's team leader also discovered that he was more successful and focused when experts had printed copies of his lab materials available for him, rather than making him work directly online with HERO. Slowly, Michael has become successful in meeting his weekly goals (lab attendance, project completion, and credit attainment), and over time his self-confidence has improved. Michael has made major improvements in the areas of his overall behavior in the lab and with his academic achievement. Prior to staff interventions, he would have multiple behavioral problems during a typical four-hour class day. In terms of his academic performance, staff focused his abilities and helped him use those abilities in the lab. Michael has made vast academic strides over the past two years, earning more than 12 lab credits. He is now working on completing his final three courses, needing only two credits to graduate. Michael still has "bad" days, but overall, he shows steady signs of improvement as he nears graduation. He has completed his FAFSA application and has been accepted to Mott Community College. He plans on operating his own business one day.

Jackson: Overcoming a History of School Suspension

Jackson is a 14-year-old researcher who enrolled in W-A-Y with a total of 3.5 middle school credits. He transferred to W-A-Y after having multiple behavioral issues and suspensions at his previous charter school, including a long-term suspension for being involved in a fight at his school. It was evident that his behavioral struggles were going to continue. Jackson had considerable difficulties getting involved with his school work. He spent much of his time in the lab avoiding his work and became immediately upset and defensive when talked to regarding his lab behavior.

Multiple parent meetings and sometimes daily phone calls home slowly turned into a successful strategy to help him improve his lab behavior. He would begin each day by meeting with his team leader and they would discuss his goals for the week. Jackson knew that his mother called the lab on a weekly basis to check on his progress and often times she would stop in to the lab to see how his day went. Distractions were also removed from his learning environment to help him move forward with his schooling.

One of the greatest challenges for Jackson was becoming comfortable with the process of using the online HERO learning system and understanding the steps necessary to complete a project from beginning to end. After several one-on-one conferences about HERO, he began to feel more comfortable with it. Jackson began doubling and tripling his weekly program goals and in less than one and a half years he has transitioned into the high school environment where he continues to excel weekly and has earned more than 1.50 credits in less than two months.

Prior to interventions, Jackson had been removed from the learning environment multiple times due to excessive talking and not following lab rules. After the interventions described above, he has not had a single behavioral referral in nearly a year. Focusing on his strengths and providing individualized instruction, such as Title I Math Services, has helped him continue to be successful in the W-A-Y program. In the past year and a half, he has completed both the 7th and 8th grade as well as earning more than 1.50 high school credits. He is well on his way to being a very successful researcher.

THE RESEARCHERS SPEAK

The best way to grasp the positive impact W-A-Y is having on the lives of those being educated in a W-A-Y site is to talk with them. What follows are unedited quotes from conversations with W-A-Y researchers. Their conversations were with James Bosco. None of those with whom he spoke knew him. The researchers he spoke with were those who were available when he was at two of the Academies. The conversations were informal. The purpose they serve here is to give an approximation of what someone could hear if they, like him, walked into a W-A-Y site and spoke with some of the researchers. We begin with Corrine and Robert whose profiles were provided above.

Corrine

"I came to W-A-Y Academy with 9.5 credits. I am the oldest sibling and am trying to be a great role model for my siblings. Since January 9, 2017, I have met my attendance requirement and have finished two core classes. I often get off task when my friends are around; however, I am never disrespectful when redirected by staff.

Intervention is not always necessary for me because I try my hardest to be a very respectful young lady when adults ask me to do something. I am very receptive and do not give staff any negative feedback. My academic goal was to improve myself as a person because if I progress as a person I will improve in my academics. I am not on track to graduate at this point, but if I continue to work hard I will be on target.

In less than a month, I have completed two of my core classes and my attendance has improved. If I can finish two core classes in two months I can graduate from W-A-Y Academy at my expected graduation date. I want to graduate and become a teacher so that I can help students, like my teachers at W-A-Y Academy help me."

Robert

"When I was at [my other school] it felt like school work got piled up and piled up. My anxiety was so bad that I didn't even want to open my computer. I felt I was going to throw up every single time I thought about school. It got really overwhelming because they were like 'Oh you have two hours of every class,' and it's like I get really sick and I can't do stuff most days. So, when those two hours each day pile up it's like eight hours for one class because I missed. It's entirely too much. At that point, I felt it wasn't a realistic goal to graduate high school. The [W-A-Y] lab works better [than a totally online school experience] for me because the schedule is really flexible for me and I can come in the mornings if I have to or I can come in the afternoons. It's a lot better than a conventional school day because I have a lot of doctor's appointments, along with being sick. The school adapts to me. Before, when I got something wrong, it would be immediately pointed out and that was a really big basis for my anxiety about school. Now I am not afraid about being wrong. That's how I learn. I know I am going to college. My parents didn't go to college and they said, 'You're going to learn from our mistakes.' I am going to go to college and I am thinking about going into electrical engineering because I have been apart of the robotics team for like a year. I thought I was not smart enough to join robotics but then I was give Paula as my mentor and she's like, 'You should join robotics.' I thought I wasn't smart enough to join robotics. And I said, 'I guess.' And I ended up liking a lot about robotics."

Eddie

"I'm trying really hard. It's kind of like, some of the stuff is really hard, but you gotta do what you gotta do. The adults will help you [researchers] get you up in your grade. They really help you and get you *there*. You know what I mean? Like sometimes you gotta do what you gotta do to get up there. I started this year trying to help myself because I used to be a lot worse than I am right now. I used to do a lot of really bad things, but I am trying to get my past behind me. My brother who had very good grades is now in jail, my father and grandfather passed away last year and he [Eddie's brother] couldn't handle it anymore. So, I had to put my past behind me. Go to college. Get the money and help my mom and all my family that needs to be helped."

Bob

"It's [W-A-Y] just right for me, compared to my [previous school] that was a pain. But this school is right for me. I like the school. I like the students. I like the teachers. Everybody is, like, together. It's like they accept everyone. I told my mom I was going to enter college. I want to major in criminal justice. Here, I am basically teaching myself. I think because anytime I needed help, they'd help me and I'd understand and go back and do another project by myself. Like when I was struggling in math here, there was a teacher named Mr. X and he helped me. I got it good. Some of the other teachers would help. Teachers help me when I need it. I feel the teachers are here for the students. They aren't here just to make money off us."

Marco

"Well, first I started off to graduate in 2014 from an online school. And in 2014, after I had graduated and stuff, I took the year off school, was working and trying to get into the military. And last year after I took a year off to just work and stuff, I tried to enter the Navy. They had said that the diploma was fake. So it was two years that I was off school. If it was told to me earlier I could have taken advantage of it, but the online school had stolen the money that I had invested in it. The Navy tried to help me. They said if I could find any proof of the school still being there, but I couldn't find anything. Everything happened to be deleted. Then the BBB, Better Business Bureau, the rankings of the school and all the reviews of it were terrible so it was something that I didn't look into and I paid for it so now I'm trying to make up for the lost time.

At first, I wanted to [quit], I'm not going to lie. It wasn't easy. It was hard, the first few months with it. But I want to be somebody. I know it was a mistake I made so I had to make up for it and at the end of the day everything is a learning experience. Potentially this will be a story that I will tell one day [to anyone] that probably goes through the same thing that I went through. And I want a better life than as I grew up. I want to be able to take care of my family and hopefully be somebody by the time I graduate.

Honestly my performance here, the few months that I have been here, has been amazing. The staff has helped me on anything that I needed, and I felt like it's something that you can't fake. Because sometimes you can go places and see that certain teachers are not really caring and not involved, and I've had teachers here since I've been here that always greet me when I come in. That's the good thing I think. Stuff like getting greeted with good morning. They're always making sure that I'm doing what I have to do and they go the extra mile for me and that's something that you don't find everywhere. Somebody that will go the extra mile for you without knowing you is something. That's amazing. So that's what I would tell somebody that's trying to come here. Do what you have to do and the teachers here are to support you. That's something you don't find everywhere [in his other schools.] It's like the students are there for the teachers rather than the teachers there for the students."

STAFF PERSPECTIVES

A questionnaire was sent to staff at the same time as questionnaires were sent to researchers. It contained several open-ended questions, including questions about what they liked about working at W-A-Y and any features of W-A-Y that they considered to be particularly important in the operation of the Program. The responses from staff were anonymous. A number of staff members wrote about the positive consequences of personalization and expressed appreciation for being able to work with W-A-Y researchers as individuals. One staff member wrote that W-A-Y enables staff members to help researchers to "identify career possibilities based on their interests and talents, exposing them to professionals in their chosen fields of study and interests, and sharing life experiences that help them make sense of things going on in their world/lives". Another staff member reported that staff members "get to build a school that puts the needs of the student over everything else."

A number of staff members commented on the relationships between researchers and staff. The W-A-Y Program intended to provide a social climate that was quite different from that which exists in the typical school. Staff members commented on this situation: "WAY is very flexible. The students have many ways to get from point a to point b, not just 'my way or the highway' type of mentality"; "I love how much easier it is to build strong relationships with students and better meet their needs as learners"; "I get to build a school that puts the needs of the student above everything else.

The survey contained a question that asked staff about what they particularly enjoyed as a W-A-Y staff member. Some responses were: "Being a part of something amazing and cutting edge to help young people who would otherwise fall through the cracks"; "When I get a breakthrough with a researcher, or have someone graduate that was never successful in other types of programs"; "Working in a learning community that is immersive"; "Access to great teachers for collaboration, and being able to talk to students one-on-one in a way that is beneficial for them. Beneficial for me most of the time too!"; "I love the people I work with and it's a great feeling to be a part of an organization that is really making a difference in young people's lives"

STAFF MEMBERS SPEAK

The staff members who are quoted below are quite representative of the W-A-Y personnel. They are added here to provide a bit more texture to the more abstract information/questionnaire data presented above.

Tim

"There are differences here compared to a traditional environment. Here we are not isolated into classrooms and it creates this space where we are all surrounded by each other constantly. Sometimes I can feel a little friction. Anyone can just walk up at any time, but it puts us all together. The student-teacher [relationship] is a lot closer than it is in a traditional classroom where you see a kid for an hour and then they are off to another class and same with my relationship with my administrators and things like that.

"We have more of a tighter knit here. It's really a safe space. All the students come in knowing it's a safe space. They know they have their mentor who they can talk to if they need anything. It creates this open environment in terms of the conversations we have and how the students are receptive to us. I really like what we do here. Kids who come here thinking it is going to be easy are the ones who stall for months before they get on board. If you are doing it [project based learning] appropriately, you are having an authentic experience and that's going to require rigor because students know they are going to have to showcase this piece. The most important thing is that here we use a student-centered model that also tries to establish an authentic community experience. I think the project based learning is important to me. The mentoring role keeps it really student centered. I don't think I would teach without PBL anymore. If someday I went back to a classroom I think I would still use a PBL model. I don't see any other way that is as engaging or effective."

Samantha

"So this [the job interview with W-A-Y] was only my second interview. My first was at, I can't remember the name of the school, but it was a very well-to-do school out in suburbia somewhere. It was kind of a drive from my house, and it went really well. Actually, when he called me back he was like, 'You made this very difficult for us, we really thought we had our mind made up when you walked in, but you made us rethink everything, but you had no experience. So we had to go with this other candidate, but we will keep you in mind.' And then this (the interview with W-A-Y) was my second interview, and I almost didn't even take the interview because I was kind of anti-charters at the time.

"So I did some research and I started reading, and I was like, wow this sounds very different. It sounds more student centered, which I'm a big believer in, and it sounds like the students might actually have a voice in what's going on. So I came for the interview, and there was a student who sat in my interview. And I was really impressed by that. And they asked him before the interview, 'Do you have any questions for her?' And I heard them asking for his feedback. And that was actually what sealed the deal when they called for a second interview, I was like, I'm going, because of the student being in the interview. I kind of liked that it [W-A-Y] wasn't as traditional because I feel like it opens up for more creativity on the instructor part too, which is important, especially when you have hard to reach kids."

Anna

"I feel like so many of them [W-A-Y researchers] didn't succeed in their other schools because they were so textbook type schools in the traditional sense of learning, and [in W-A-Y they] actually had a different perspective. They were able to create something, and do something hands on rather than, 'Study this. Regurgitate it for a test.' When I was there [in the school where she previously worked], I had to pretend I wasn't so poor, and here it really doesn't matter. It actually helps me. I didn't grow up with a lot of money, and it helps me to be able to relate to the kids who are struggling too."

Paula

"Well, in both of those settings [where she previously taught] I had much larger class sizes. I really wanted something different. I wanted a much smaller group of kids to work with at a time because it was really overwhelming. In [the school where she previously taught] I'd have forty something kids in a room which is so ridiculous to think that I could meet all of their needs. And then, the second school was supposed to have smaller groups, but I was an elective teacher. I taught Spanish then, and so my classes weren't the same as the core classes they could keep smaller, but mine were still in the thirties. So, I really wanted something drastically smaller.

I didn't really have an interest in working in that setting. That's where I grew up and I feel I was pretty ignorant of realities outside of where I was. And then once I started to learn about it, probably through sociology class in my high school, I started to realize that there is a huge problem of inequality. I was lucky enough to not realize that before because I was kind of isolated in a bubble. And then once I went to Michigan State, that's where I went to school to become a teacher, a lot of our classes were about sociology and education. And I wanted to be part of the solution to the vast inequality. Just the fact that a lot of teachers maybe feel like a stigma about students like that or they don't understand that they need something different. I think just about any kid could benefit from a different approach from just traditional 'read this, answer these questions' type approach to education. Especially kids in that setting, it doesn't work at all. So I thought that I could learn methods that would help students in that setting.

I think it helps to try to understand where they're coming from. So, a lot of times especially at the beginning of the school year I'll talk to them about what their previous education experiences have been like and ask them on surveys questions like, 'How do you feel about reading?' And a lot of times they'll say, 'I hate reading. I've never read a book, I just pretend like I'm reading books in school.' And so, understanding why they might feel that way by talking to them could kind of help me figure out a different approach for them."

SIDEBAR

At the beginning of this chapter it was mentioned that the best way to get a good and compelling perspective of what W-A-Y at "ground level" is to enter a W-A-Y site and observe what is happening and talk with researchers and staff. That is exactly what the team from AdvancED did in conjunction with the 2017 accreditation of W-A-Y. AdvancEd (described in Chapter One) is one of the major educational accreditation organizations in the world. Including some excerpts from their report is a good way to end this chapter:

"The External Review Team conducted 12 classroom observations that represented a good balance of grade levels, content areas, and locations. WAY corporation's averages were higher than the AdvancED Network Average in all seven learning environments. Amongst the seven learning environments, the school achieved the highest level in the Well-Managed Learning Environment and Active Learning Environment with both having an average rating of 3.28 [on a four-point scale]. In addition, the quality of the learning environments was evident in the Supportive Learning Environment, which rated 3.23, followed by Progress Monitoring and Feedback environment at an average rating of 3.22. The learning environment as a whole was very positive, where students expressed positive attitude about their experiences in teaching and learning, and the support they receive to master content, competencies and skills. These various characteristics within the Supportive Learning Environment achieved an average rating of 3.05."

The external review team from AdvancED that conducted the 2017 accreditation of W-A-Y found "numerous aspects of best practices in the observed classrooms. They reported that "W-A-Y has an outstanding teaching staff" and that "It was evident that teachers built strong relationships with their students and the lessons were truly student-centered" (citation). They observed that "parents and other stakeholders shared that they have overwhelming pride in the school and that students are learning based on their own interest in such a wonderful, supportive setting" (citation). The classroom atmosphere was described by students to the AdvancEd team as "family and caring," and where students felt they "are getting a second chance to succeed" (citation). The team heard from many of the teachers they interviewed that "my students tell me that they love school now" and that one staff person's "love of teaching has returned due to the WAY instructional model" (citation)."The AdvancED team stated, "In the course of our interviews with mentors, team leaders, experts, students, and parents, it was clear that W-A-Y staff knows students well and advocates for their learning and growth." One of the most positive of

AdvancEd's observations was that "passion and enthusiasm appeared as a driving force within all of the observed environments" (citation).

IN CONCLUSION

It would be a mistake to conclude that every W-A-Y student and every W-A-Y staff member is happy with their involvement with W-A-Y. There is no doubt that there are students who are not satisfied with W-A-Y, as well as that there are disgruntled staff members. Yet, those persons comprise a small number of those participating in W-A-Y as staff or students. The preponderance of W-A-Y students recognize that they are experiencing schooling in a very different setting. It is a setting where, as one student put it, the teachers are here for the students rather than the students being here for the teachers. Given the fact that many of the W-A-Y students consider their experience in their previous school(s) a failure, it is quite positive to hear them speak of their current sense of empowerment as students. They now see themselves as having a positive future.

While some teachers would have difficulty accepting the way teachers in W-A-Y function, the W-A-Y staff members derive professional satisfaction as teachers who provide support and guidance in assisting students to accomplish the learning goals they have set for themselves. Teachers take personal satisfaction in seeing how the W-A-Y experience can have a positive impact on students.

As one interacts with W-A-Y researchers, it becomes quite clear that the explanations of some school personnel, policy makers, and citizens for the reason behind problems young people have in school are as vacuous as they are false. One excuse might be, "They just do not like school." While it is true that many of the young people who come to W-A-Y would say they do not like school, their dislike of school is not wired into their minds; it is an acquired belief caused by the bad experiences they have had. When someone is repeatedly told they are not good at something eventually they will give up and probably leave the situation, with a strong negative opinion about it. Not liking school is the not the cause, but the consequence, of many of these students' experience. Others may say, "They just are not smart enough." Many of the young people in W-A-Y could seemingly be characterized by that statement, but the validity of it is contradicted by what can be seen when one examines the quality of work that W-A-Y researchers produce.

This chapter provided a sense of what the visitor to a W-A-Y site would encounter. It is an all-too-common situation in schools for teachers and administrators to have one perspective on the learning environment of the schools and student satisfaction with it, and for the students to have a different perspective. Conversations with W-A-Y teachers and researchers show a high degree of convergence between researcher and staff opinions and give confidence that W-A-Y's founding goals are being met. The researchers and staff members whose voices were heard in this chapter are hardly unique. Without prompting, those within the W-A-Y community will focus on the factors that were critical in the design of W-A-Y. Hearing from the people who are at "ground zero" confirms the belief that it is possible to meet the challenge and seize the opportunity to make high school work for our young people.

FIVE

Summing Up and Moving Forward

Glen and Beth do not have many opportunities to take a deep breath, sit down, and reflect on the work they have done over the past several years. This chapter gives them a chance to do so. Through an interview with the author, Jim Bosco, they look back at what they have learned and accomplished, as well as what lies ahead.

Jim: The two of you have been educators for about three decades and partners in the work directly related to W-A-Y for about a decade. It was what you saw happening to a large number of youth in the U.S., and particularly in Michigan, that motivated you to get involved. How much progress have we made as a nation and as a state from when you began to the present moment?

Beth: Certainly not as much progress as we should have made, but there has been some progress. When we started, little was being said or done with regard to practices that are now embedded in W-A-Y, such as blended learning, cross curricula learning, and the removal of the time constraints on student learning. Those ideas were new for many of those with whom we spoke eight years ago. This was so not just for alternative ed students, but for all students. You could talk about those concepts with education experts or professors; yet, when we were working with those who we needed to understand what we were proposing, such as to school boards, parents, or with school personnel, those concepts were new and strange and perhaps a bit scary.

It is much easier to have those conversations now than it was then. Now people generally know what we are talking about when we describe the main components of W-A-Y, but it's still a challenge getting to an understanding of what it takes to actually embed those practices in the learning environment. The task is not to add these elements to the existing school structure. The task is to use those elements to make fundamental changes in how teaching and learning occurs for our young people. Some who appear to be on the same page, are only paying lip service to those concepts or seeking to make use of those elements in a way that does not seriously change established practice.

Jim: Glen?

Glen: As a nation and as a state we are not where we need to be. Many of those who say they want to increase options for students have done so only on the surface. We are not doing enough to really engage kids, to stop them from wanting to leave school and actually leaving or feeling as though their school doesn't have their best interest at heart.

Beth made an important point with regard to how innovations are often treated in the educational community. She mentioned "blended learning." Too often that just means that the teacher puts a lesson on the Internet, so students can watch it at home and then discuss it in class. So now they can watch a lecture at home rather than at school. "Innovations" can be used to do pretty much what we have been doing in schools for decades.

We get our cake and eat it too! We can claim to be "innovative" while still keeping things pretty much the same.

We realize we're not the only people in the U.S. who are seriously trying to widen advancement for our youth. Unfortunately, what we've often seen in this work over the last eight years is that those who are implementing innovations fall back to the old way of doing things. They try it on for a short time and the system makes it very difficult to sustain the innovation. The innovation either dies or is "sanitized" to fit into the status-quo. The innovation should have a chance to work and to get the "bugs" out, which takes time and persistence.

Jim: In your answer to the first question, you named issues and problems, concerns, that are hampering our ability to do the best we can for our kids. If you could put your finger on one obstacle you consider to be at the top of the list, what would that be?

Glen: Our education system in the U.S. does not have a good way to assess and put value on addressing the whole child, their social wellbeing, and all the different aspects of creating awesome human beings who we need to lead this world. Our main way to assess how well we are doing the job in our schools is through high-stakes testing. Those tests don't tell the whole story. We don't have a reason to be defensive about our students' test scores but seeing our students from the window of their test scores, as some believe to be the best or only way to see them, gives a distorted and incomplete sense of who they are, what they have accomplished, and where they are headed. This is one of the things that we've had the most difficult time communicating, particularly to policy makers. As we talk about our students in that vein we hear, too often, "Yes that is really great, but what are their test scores?"

Beth: What Glen mentioned is a big barrier. Another big obstacle is that many structures and practices that we put into our schools make schools work for the school personnel, but not necessarily for the kids. We often hear school personnel say, "Kids come first," but in reality, too often they come second. We need to recognize that we have failed them, and that it will take clear thinking and good actions to bring our young people to their full potential. And we shouldn't throw our hands up and give up on them because they are 16.

Jim: From what you both have said it is clear that this work requires people of a certain type. What qualities, characteristics, and dispositions should people have in order to have a fighting chance at success along the same lines that WAY has been working?

Beth: I think it is necessary to have a sense of urgency. I heard over and over again, "Let's take our time and get this right." Rather than being a call for action, that is actually an excuse for inaction. Oftentimes we hear that we have to go slow to go fast. We have to take five steps back to take two steps forward. When you start with that idea, you've already handicapped yourself. Moving fast does not mean that this is done without a good understanding of the problem. It is necessary to know what are the causes and what are the effects and to use that understanding to come up with the best possible solutions. As you move forward it is critical to check yourself, move forward, check yourself, altering and refining what you are implementing as needed. Altering your path based on practice and data is not stepping backwards; you're still moving forward.

The starting point for us was to face the fact that we have far too many of our young people in Michigan dropping out of school. They're dropping out because school is not relevant to their lives. We had to get past that generality and come to a better understanding of the issues beneath the generality and to create a learning environment that is really relevant to the students in it.

We had many people who were ready and able to give us negative feedback consistently. You have to have the capacity to say, "This person has the best interests of children at heart. I need to step back and listen, even though it's not something I want to hear." In other cases, it was clear that the person giving the criticism was doing so to keep the status-quo. But even then, it is important to listen to what is being said, but to not weaken your commitment to solving the problem. It is important to be curious and always to be on the lookout, no matter from what source, for what can be learned to make things work better. I don't think you're born with the ability to deal with criticism in that manner; I think life helps us to develop that attitude.

Glen: We set out to try to change education, not for the teachers and other adults on the staff, but ultimately for the kids. We would try things and they would work fairly well, but we kept looking for how to make our practices convergent with our vision. As long you hold true to the vision it can be achieved; how you achieve the vision can change and develop over time. It is important to listen to the stakeholders that you're serving and make the corrections that are needed. If you continually do that, you will arrive at something very powerful. It becomes more difficult to achieve a clear vision when there's other influencers such as foundations offering money, but in taking that money you're now also accepting their vision, their path. We knew what we wanted to achieve, and we stayed focused. We stayed focused on building the software that we needed, assessing the structures and policies we put in place to make sure we were not creating our own obstacles to success, and monitoring how teachers were interacting with our students. You can ask any of our teachers or administrators about our goal and they would say that the fundamental aspect of W-A-Y was to make our students have a great experience, educationally and socially, and that they feel cared for and engaged. As we've expanded as an organization, as a network, those are goals that we've held steadfast to and it's proved to be right.

Jim: Let me ask you another question. What did you face in the development of WAY that surprised you, both positive and negative?

Glen: The level of animosity, sometimes aggression, and dealing with the obstacles that are put in your way as you try to do right by kids. That took us a while to get used to. It was not unusual for us to hear from people, "No. It's impossible. You can't do it like this. You can't do that." And we'd figure out ways to do it. It surprised us quite a bit when people said to us things like, "Those kids really shouldn't have another chance." And, "Wow. You're going to put computers in those kids' homes? That shouldn't happen." And they would go as far to even swear at us sometimes, telling us they can't believe that we could be so reckless. We were naive in thinking that everyone would want us to succeed. Facing up to this was one of the most difficult things that we had to overcome

Jim: And that surprised you?

Glen: It sure did.

Beth: And I have to agree with Glen. He's saying "animosity," I would even say the level of hatred that was thrown at us. We had some pretty tough times based on people's prejudices. They saw us as people that wanted to do harm to the public-school system, and that couldn't be farther from the truth. We believe in the public-school system. Yet we also absolutely believe that each young person should have the very best education we can provide, not just "good enough," but the best.

I thought that people would help pick up the banner and walk with us, but it was a lonely walk. The people who were the most supportive were actually business owners, and specifically small business owners. They really understood what we were doing and why we were doing it. We also got support from citizens and parents who told us stories of their own experiences in school and who would say, "If only this was around when I was in school." We did face harsh criticism and animosity from educators, but we also had many prospective teachers and administrators who would say, "Oh my gosh. This is exactly what I would want to participate in. This is exactly what I would want to be doing."

The other big surprise to me was what we saw at our graduations. With our partner schools and with the charter schools, we have several graduations each year. What we experienced at our graduations just blew us away. We would have a completely full ballroom or auditorium. The number of people in the audience was far more than what you would expect for the number of graduates. The entire neighborhood, you know, extended family members, everybody showed up to support this young person who was graduating. That was a big, wonderful surprise as well. It showed that what we were doing in W-A-Y was important to the community as well as the students. That's why I want to look at what's next, because our young people aren't just influencing their own lives, but they're influencing the lives of their neighbors, of their own siblings, of their parents, of their own children for some of them. I see that vividly when I go to our graduations. Our students have such strength, and to be able to help unleash those into the world is why I became part of all of this.

Glen: Another good surprise has been how well things have gone with W-A-Y being in private schools, in charter schools, and in public schools. And they're all working together in the same organizational environment and having no problem. I think that's been a pleasant surprise, you know? It's not something that you would anticipate.

Beth: Yes, that was a very good surprise. Originally, we didn't think that we could have charter schools, and private schools, and traditional schools all in one learning environment, but it's made it stronger and it has worked out well.

Jim: There were some big "ups" and some big "downs." My question is: what has been your biggest satisfaction as a result of your work with W-A-Y? What is it that makes you feel good about coming to work every morning? Beth?

Beth: I love the feeling of, "What's next?" I love to be able to walk in, make an assessment, and think about what's next. What are we going to do that's going to help our young people learn? What are we going to develop that's going to really allow our staff to connect with our students and their families? I just love being able to have the luxury at this point, to be able to take a step back and look at the progress and then look at where we're going next.

Jim: Glen?

Glen: I just had a conversation with my son just the other day. He said, "I want to have a job that I really love. Do you love your job?" I said, "Yes I do. I love the work we do every day. We get to deal with matters that are very important and change the world for a lot of kids. We've touched a lot of kids, and a lot of families."

It's exciting work. We have a plethora of opportunities for the organization and we have wonderful staff members that work with us. They have committed their careers to what we seek to accomplish. We've had people who have been with us for years and they enjoy their work and see that they're making a difference. Those are all really powerful pieces for an organization. The days aren't ever the same, but it's good work and we get into great conversations with those around us about how best to make the name of our organization, Widening Advancements for Youth, not just a nice name, but a reality in the lives of our students.

Jim: Let me ask you to do some "Monday morning quarterbacking" on yourself. What do you know now that you wish you had known earlier in the creation of W-A-Y?

Beth: There are so many things that would have been helpful to know ahead of time. I'm going to mention one: I wish I wasn't as dogmatic as I was at the very beginning. I think that closed me to some possible solutions, some possible partners, because I felt we should only be working with traditional public schools. I wish I had come to that open-mindedness of working with multiple types of organizations earlier.

Glen: For me, it was what was involved in running the business, which doesn't seem like that should impact the educational aspects of our work, but it impacts everything. With my responsibilities as a principal and district administrator I had needed to deal with fiscal matters, but it is quite different to do that and to run a business. Running W-A-Y as a 501(c) (3) meant that we had total responsibility for the business aspects of W-A-Y. There was a huge learning curve on our part.

Beth: We didn't fully understand the magnitude of the risk to our careers when we left our jobs at the RESA and the school district. We knew that there was risk; we just didn't understand the entire implications of taking that step that would cut our connections that we've spent a career developing. It cut us from what we knew. Yet at the same time it also allowed us to move forward, because people who respected the work that we had done in the past trusted us to help them move forward as well. In hindsight we can now say, "Wow, that was a huge risk." Both of us didn't know that we were completely cutting ourselves off from the career paths that we had left behind.

Jim: What are the ingredients, the key ingredients, that are required to create a learning environment that really works for the clientele that you are serving in W-A-Y? Are those ingredients the same as what you think would be effective and valuable to a broader audience, the kids who right now are sitting in our traditional, conventional high schools? Glen?

Glen: The elements we have focused on such as personalized learning, cross-curricular learning, project based learning would absolutely be relevant for any student. All students would find it very good to have a say in what the curriculum is, and what interests them as a student. Certainly, any student could benefit from a learning environment where they can go back and revise their work. It is great to see students working in an environment where they realize they don't have to just move on because the bell rang but can keep working until they accomplish the goals of the learning at hand.

We are showing that such an approach works in public schools, private schools, charter schools, and alternative schools. It kind of bumps up against the traditional, more structured settings. We try to create environments that are not as structured. Managing thirty students in a very specific, constrained amount of time poses a very difficult problem even for the best of teachers. Allowing students to have the amount of time they need to accomplish any learning task results in deeper learning and encourages that student engagement. The teacher may be as aware as we are about how to make the school work better for their students, but, for example, if that teacher has thirty kids in their class, it is likely that they are going to teach to the middle twenty and they'll lose some on the top and lose some on the bottom, either the ability to engage farther, or to modify things to fit the learner that would learn better in another way.

Beth: Your question was about what the components are for a learning environment and will they work all students or just, only specifically with the W-A-Y program students? I would say that good practice is good practice, and it doesn't matter with whom you're working, adults or young people.

When you look at what learners' needs are, and what are best practices to support their learning, we know that they need to be able to make connections between what they learn in school and what they experience in their real life. One of the ways to make those connections is to ensure that students have voice and choice and to have a curriculum that is modifiable, or even, if possible, co-constructed. Project based learning is one of the modalities that works well in order to make real connections in a cross-curricular context. The projects are modifiable to respond to the needs and interests of students, while still meeting the state standards. We know that many of the competencies aligned with our projects are going to help our young people achieve on our standardized tests. Do we want to set up an entire system around testing? No. Nevertheless, we know that our young people will be taking standardized tests. We'd do a disservice to our learners to not align the projects to the competencies as embodied in the standards.

Using PBL does not mean that students will score poorly on state tests; the opposite is true. Whether we agree with all of the standards or not doesn't matter. It's what our society is asking us to ensure that our young people learn while they're in school. It is not good to be confined to one pre-packaged, unmodifiable system to implement the curriculum. When you accept a textbook as your curriculum, you're setting yourself up for a lot of hardship and your learning environment to be much less effective but choosing between meeting standards or providing students with learning that is functional in their lives does not have to be an either/or choice.

Let me add one other point. In education, I don't want to be limited to thinking about learning only inside of schools, because our young people are going to have more and more learning resources available to them. If we're really looking at focusing on doing what is right for our kids, we shouldn't be only focusing on what happens inside the walls of schools. Schools should be a place where our students develop a capacity to use the vast array of resources that are available, many at no cost, on the

Internet. We need to make the walls of the school more permeable, not only in virtual space, but in real space as well. Why can't more schools make use of an approach we have in one of our schools that's opening up near Detroit? It's actually inside of a warehouse that has manufacturing, and we have engineers that get released time to come and work with the young people.

There's just a lot of different ways that learning can happen and our education systems should take full advantage of this. None of us know the totality of what learning opportunities will look like in the next three to five years. We do know that there will be more and more opportunities for learning in many venues of society. And, thus far, a traditional school with a learning environment that has been more or less the same for many, many years is not the answer.

Jim: Glen?

I am excited to share what we've done and what we can do in education with people with whom we have a shared ethos and a strong commitment to making substantial progress in making our schools do a better job for our students. We got into this years ago to really try to change public education and that is a heavy lift. We are not alone, and while there is still much to be learned and accomplished, there has been progress. We are confident we are on the right path. We are happy to contribute all we can to create an education that works.

Moving Forward

Earlier in this book, we spoke of a crisis facing our nation. This crisis results from the large number of American youths who do not receive an education that prepares them for their future. This certainly pertains to those young people who leave high school without a diploma, but it also extends beyond them. In the world of today, just having a diploma is not good enough to put our young people on a path to advance their lives in a positive direction. Our youth need to have the knowledge and capabilities needed for a good career when they leave school. When this does not happen, it is not only a loss for the individual student, but a loss of the talent and energy from those who could contribute to the well-being of their local communities and the nation. We need educators who are in a position to respond to the crisis to roll up their sleeves and face the tough challenge of making the needed transformational changes in our schools.

This book told the story of how W-A-Y came to be and what it has accomplished in the nine years of its existence. Beth and Glen do not believe they have *the* answer for what is needed to make education work for all our young people, but they believe they have *an* answer.

W-A-Y is making education work for the young people who are participating in the Program. At the same time, Beth and Glen recognize that they, like all who are engaged in these efforts, need to continue to learn what works and what does not work as they engage in the continuing improvement of the W-A-Y program. They align themselves with others in many places across the nation who are similarly committed to making big changes in the school experience for our young people. They share their work in the form of this book to encourage others to continue working for positive transformation and to show that what needs to happen, can happen.

So, we end with a call to action. We align ourselves with others who, like us, are responding to the crisis. And we understand that often those who are doing this work may experience more resistance than support for their efforts. While we may be approaching the problem in different ways, we all need to be informed about what is being done and to see ourselves not as "lone wolves," but as a cadre of committed educators who are determined to continue to confront the issues that narrow, rather than widen, the advancement of our youth.

REFERENCES

CHAPTER TWO

1 Diplomas Count 2016 Map: Graduation Rates by State, Student Group. Retrieved from: http://www.edweek.org/ew/dc/2016/map-graduation-rates-by-state-demographics.html?intc=EW-DC16-TOC

2 Nation's Graduation Rate Reaches New Record High. Retrieved from: https://www.washingtonpost.com/news/education/wp/2016/10/17/nations-high-schoo l-graduation-rate-reaches-new-record-high/?utm_term=.3a2b111656d9

3 Diplomas Count 2016 Map: Graduation Rates by State, Student Group. Retrieved from: http://www.edweek.org/ew/dc/2016/map-graduation-rates-by-state-demographics.html?intc=EW-DC16-TOC

   Diplomas Count. (2015). Michigan: Next Steps After Special Education. Retrieved from: http://www.edweek.org/media/ew/dc/2015/sgb/33sgb.mi.h34.pdf

4 America's Promise Alliance. Cities in Crisis. Retrieved from: http://www.americaspromise.org/cities-crisis

   Kids Count Data Center. Retrieved from http://datacenter.kidscount.org/

5 Diplomas Count 2016 Map: Graduation Rates by State, Student Group. Retrieved from: http://www.edweek.org/ew/dc/2016/map-graduation-rates-by-state-demographics.html?intc=EW-DC16-TOC

America's Promise Alliance. Cities in Crisis. Retrieved from http://www. americaspromise.org/cities-crisis

6   Diplomas Count. (2015). Michigan: Next Steps After Special Education. Retrieved from http://www.edweek.org/media/ew/dc/2015/sgb/33sgb.mi.h34.pdf

7   Rowe, C. (Jan. 3, 2014). Seattle Times: Education Lab Blog. Retrieved from http://blogs.seattletimes.com/educationlab/2014/01/03/how-much-do-dropout s-cost-us-the-real-numbers-behind-pay-now-or-pay-later/

8   National Center for Educational Statistics. Retrieved from https://nces.ed.gov/ fastfacts/display.asp?id=77,

9   Freudenberg, Nicholas, Ruglis, Jessica. (2007}. Reframing School Dropout as a Public Health Problem. Retrieved from http://www.cdc.gov/pcd/issues/2007/ oct/07_0063.htm

10   Parsons, C. (1989). Dropout Darwinism: School Counselors Helping the Fittest, Abandoning the Rest. Retrieved from: http://articles.latimes.com/1989-07-02/ opinion/op-4600_1_college-guidance-counselors

11   Knesting, Kimberly, Lund, Dustin, Reese, Robert Brody. (2013) Influence On Students' Decisions To Stay In Or dropout of school. Journal of Studies in Education. Vol. 3, No. 4 p57.

12   Rees, N. (2005). The tragedy of our near-million high-school dropout rate, and how to end it. Retrieved from http://hechingerreport.org/the-tragedy-of-ou r-near-million-high-school-dropout-rate-and-how-to-end-it/

13   Arizona Department of Education. High School Graduation Requirements. Retrieved from http://www.azed.gov/hsgraduation/

14   Jordan W. J., Lara J., McPartland J. M. (1994). Exploring the complexity of early dropout causal structures. Baltimore, MD: Center for Research on Effective Schooling for Disadvantaged Students. Retrieved from http://files. eric.ed.gov/fulltext/ED375227.pdf

15   Doll, J, Eslami, Z, and Walters, L. (2013). Zohreh Eslami, Lynne Walters. Understanding Why Students Drop Out of High School According To Their Own Reports. Retrieved from http://journals.sagepub.com/doi/ abs/10.1177/2158244013503834

16   National School Boards Association, Center for Public Education. Keeping Kids in School: What Research Tells about Preventing Dropouts._____ http://www.centerforpubliceducation.org/system/files/ Keeping_kids_in_school_FullReport.pdf

17 Born This Way Foundation. Retrieved from https://bornthisway.foundation/emotionrevolution/summit/

18 Aspen Institute. (2005). Students', Teachers', and Administrators' Attitudes Towards High School and School Reform. Retrieved from: https://assets.aspeninstitute.org/content/uploads/files/content/docs/education/educationteacherviews.pdf

19 The Glossary of Educational Reform: School Culture. Retrieved from: https://www.edglossary.org/school-culture/

20 Tuck, K. D. (1989). A study of students who left: Washington, D.C. public school dropouts. Paper presented at the annual conference of the American Education Research Association, San Francisco.

21 Young, T. W. (1990). Public alternative education: Options and choice for today's schools. New York: Teachers College Press.

22 Kerr, K. & Legters, N. (2004). Preventing dropout: Use and impact of organizational reforms designed to ease the transition to high school in Dropouts in America. Edited by Gary Orfield. Cambridge, MA: Harvard Education Press, 238.

23 Lawler, P.A. (1991). The Keys To Adult Learning: Theory and Practical Strategies. Philadelphia: Research for Better Schools. Retrieved from: https://files.eric.ed.gov/fulltext/ED345108.pdf

24 Department of Education. (1994). National education commission on time and learning. Washington, DC: Retrieved from: https://eric.ed.gov/?id=ED489343

25 Reynolds, Ruth. THE Journal. The Changing Role of Instructors Moving from Facilitation to Constructive Partnerships. Retrieved from: https://thejournal.com/articles/2010/04/07/the-changing-role-of-instructors-moving-from-facilitation-to-constructive-partnerships.aspx

CHAPTER THREE

1 Michigan Merit Curriculum. Retrieved from: http://www.michigan.gov/documents/mde/Complete_MMC_FAQ_August_2014_467323_7.pdf

2 Michigan Merit Curriculum. Earth Science https://www.michigan.gov/documents/EARTHMMC_168211_7.pdf

3 Elmbrook School District Personalized Learning. Retrieved from: https://www.elmbrookschools.org/teaching-learning/personalized-learning

4 EdSurge. Why Project based Learning Hasn't Gone Mainstream (And What We Can Do About It). Retrieved from: https://www.edsurge.com/news/2016-04-23

-why-project   based-learning-hasn-t-gone-mainstream-and-what-we-can-do-about-it

5   EdSurge. Why Project based Learning Hasn't Gone Mainstream (And What We Can Do About It). Retrieved from: https://www.edsurge.com/news/2016-04-23-why-project based-learning-hasn-t-gone-mainstream-and-what-we-can-do-about-it

www.ingramcontent.com/pod-product-compliance
Lightning Source LLC
La Vergne TN
LVHW021402080426
835508LV00020B/2405